THE GREAT PECOS MISSION 1540-2000

THE GREAT PECOS MISSION 1540-2000

Stories

Carol Paradise Decker

SANTA FE

© 2012 by Carol Paradise Decker
All Rights Reserved.

No part of this book may be reproduced in any form or by any electronic or mechanical means including information storage and retrieval systems without permission in writing from the publisher, except by a reviewer who may quote brief passages in a review.

Sunstone books may be purchased for educational, business, or sales promotional use. For information please write: Special Markets Department, Sunstone Press, P.O. Box 2321, Santa Fe, New Mexico 87504-2321.

Book and Cover design › Vicki Ahl
Body typeface › Book Antiqua
Printed on acid-free paper
∞

Library of Congress Cataloging-in-Publication Data

Decker, Carol Paradise, 1927-
  The Great Pecos mission, 1540-2000 : stories / by Carol Paradise Decker.
     p. cm.
  Includes bibliographical references.
  ISBN 978-0-86534-892-9 (softcover : alk. paper)
  1. Pueblo Indians--New Mexico--Pecos National Historical Park--History.
2. Pueblo Indians--Missions--New Mexico--Pecos National Historical Park--History. 3. Pecos National Historical Park (N.M.)--History. I. Title.
  E99.P9D33 2012
  978.9004'974--dc23
                      2012021880

WWW.SUNSTONEPRESS.COM
SUNSTONE PRESS / POST OFFICE BOX 2321 / SANTA FE, NM 87504-2321 /USA
(505) 988-4418 / ORDERS ONLY (800) 243-5644 / FAX (505) 988-1025

Contents

To the Reader _____ 9

Introduction _____ 13

Pecos Timeline _____ 17

Fray Luis _____ 19

Cicuye _____ 23

The Spanish Invaders _____ 30

The Mission Builder _____ 37

The People Divided _____ 46

Renewal and Decline _____ 51

The Two Bishops _____ 58

The Visitor, 1776 _____ 62

The Peace of Pecos _____ 69

Interlude _____ 73

Pecos Feast Days _____ 80

Return of the Ancestors ____ 84

Sources and Notes _____ 91

Notes _____ 95

To the Reader

Thousands of visitors each year view the earth-covered rubble of the Great Pecos Pueblo in New Mexico and the towering red walls of the roofless mission church that served it. The ruins, about twenty miles east of Santa Fe, are protected and interpreted by the National Park Service. Yet the story of the mission and its interaction with the native people is seldom told in any detail. It's a story that needs to be shared. This is my attempt.

A glass saucer lay in a case in a small archaeological museum near my childhood home. It held a section of human backbone with an obsidian arrowhead embedded between the vertebrae. As a youngster, I spent many hours contemplating these remnants of human conflict, wondering who those people were, how they lived, and what brought them together. They were from Pecos.

I hung over the shoulders of curators mending baskets and rebuilding colorful pots from multiple fragments. I breathed down the neck of the artist creating a diorama of the pueblo. I struggled to read the accompanying descriptions by Coronado's chronicler in 1540. I listened to Dr. Kidder, smoking his curved-stemmed pipe and telling stories of his excavations and exploits at Pecos and elsewhere to my enthralled family. This was in Andover, Massachusetts, where the Robert S. Peabody Archeological Museum (not the larger Peabody Museum at Harvard) sponsored the Pecos work.

And so, Pecos entered my consciousness early. It was surely one of the factors that led me to a lifelong enthusiasm for archaeology, anthropology, history, the Spanish Southwest, intercultural relations, and many forms of experiential education. It led me to advanced degrees in Spanish language and heritage (Columbia University, MA, 1950) and— later—Divinity, focusing on missions (Yale Divinity School, M.Div., 1977). And along the way there were many courses and hands-on experiences building on all of these areas.

Since 1980 in Santa Fe, I have been researching and providing countless mini-courses, talks and tours, generally to adults, about the heritage of the Southwest. Naturally, Pecos is one of my favorite places.

For five years, 1998-2003, I served as a National Park volunteer at Pecos. I particularly delighted in guiding visitors through the ruins of pueblo and mission, trying to help them "see" the ancient buildings and the dramatic events that impacted the people over the years. But there was never enough time for the stories I yearned to share. Some of them are now in this book.

Outstanding among the books I have found helpful in understanding the role of the mission at Pecos is *Kiva, Cross and Crown: The Pecos Indians and New Mexico 1540–1840,* by John Kessell. This is a marvelously detailed and vivid account of the context and individuals involved in the Pecos story. But it is a huge book and overwhelming for the casual reader. I refer to it often on the following pages. I'm exceedingly grateful to Dr. Kessell for his extensive research and his ability to breathe life into those far off events.

Though a few other books are listed at the end of this volume, the massive amounts of general reading about the history and heritage of New Mexico presently available are too many to even begin to list. To which I contribute my own personal contacts, experience, and observations.

As I get caught up in some of the events described, my imagination expands reported facts, but in ways that I hope are consistent with the context. And a continuing dialogue with certain characters, though only in my head, often brings unexpected and enriching insights.

I hope these pages will encourage you to learn more about these amazing people and events. And I invite you to join me as we roam the ruins at what is now the Pecos National Historical Park. Come along.

—Carol Decker

Introduction

Around the year 1300 scattered communities in the upper Pecos Valley came together to build a new town. They made house blocks three, four, sometimes five stories high out of the abundant local rock, and hauled roof timbers from the nearby mountains. They cemented the walls with mud from the creek, plastered and whitewashed them inside and out. The house blocks surrounded a large rectangular plaza and were stepped back with terraced corridors outside each doorway. Light ladders connected each level. They could be pulled up easily in times of danger, and there were no ground-level entries to the buildings. Narrow gateways controlled access to the plaza, and a low boundary wall surrounded the whole.

The new town was called Cicuye, which meant something like City of Stone.

Cicuye was situated on a low ridge, easy to defend, with broad views in all directions. A small stream, now known as Glorieta Creek, flowed through the narrow valley between the ridge and the sheer cliffs of the mesa to the west, providing water for domestic use and space for many farm plots. A large field rolled off to the east, toward the river now known as the Pecos and the hills beyond. To the north rose the mountain range now known as the Sangre de Cristos. To the south and east the way opened to the Great Plains.

The Cicuye people grew strong and prosperous. They dominated the ancient pass between the plains and the valley of the Rio Grande. Their traders traveled far and wide and hosted great trade fairs each fall in the field below the town. Their farmers cultivated the rich cropland along the creek and by the more distant river, and produced an abundance of corn, beans and squash. Their hunters roamed the hills, plains, mesas, and mountains in search of deer, elk, bear, buffalo, and other food animals. Their craftsmen fashioned quantities of useful, ornamental and sacred objects, from materials at hand or bartered, some for their own use, some for trade. Their warriors were fierce, respected, and feared throughout the area.

Cicuye was at its peak when Coronado's expedition came through in 1540-41, and fifty years later when the first colonists settled in the area now known as New Mexico. An estimated two thousand people lived at the place the Spaniards referred to as Pecos, which also means "City of Stone" in a different pueblo language. The Spaniards referred to all the native agricultural villages in the area as "pueblos," which simply means "village" in Spanish. There were some sixty of them scattered along the Rio Grande Valley and vicinity, each independent and speaking different languages. Pecos was one of the "biggest and best" that the first expeditions encountered, and it was a pueblo to be respected and reckoned with.

A major purpose of the original settlement of New Mexico was to Christianize the native people, thereby saving their heathen souls, and making them productive citizens of the great Spanish empire. During the early years of colonization, attention and limited resources were concentrated on the pueblos along the Rio Grande. It wasn't until 1616 that the Franciscan missionaries began serious work at Pecos. By 1625, the massive adobe church—the awesome pride of the region—and the connected *convento* were completed and the work of the mission was in full swing. It brought good priests and bad, saints and celebrations, peaches and wheat, mules and tools, sheep and chickens, protection and exploitation, change and conflict—and new ways of thinking about life. Some Pecos people became nominal Christians, others resisted.

This huge church was destroyed during the Pueblo Revolt of 1680. The Spaniards returned in 1692, and eventually the original church was replaced by a smaller one nestled within the old foundations. It was completed in 1717. By that time, the population of the pueblo had diminished and the mission work had lost much of its energy. In 1838, the few remaining residents left their ancestral home to join their linguistic cousins at Jemez Pueblo across the western mountains.

Like the pueblo structures themselves, the church and *convento* deteriorated, helped along by recycling anything useful and pot hunting by local Hispanic settlers and travelers along the Santa Fe Trail. Only ruins were left. Serious archaeology began in 1915, which led to renewed understanding of the importance of the site and its protection, first as a State Monument (1934), then as a National Monument (1967) and since 1990 as a National Historical Park.

For centuries, the mission has been the heart of the Pecos Pueblo, shaping and reshaping the lives of the people. Its powerful spiritual presence has hovered over the area from 1540 to this present day. But its stories are mostly buried in historical tomes, in memories, or forgotten.

The following pages attempt to recapture some of the individuals and events relating to the Pecos mission; the contexts, achievements, frustrations and conflicts; the rich swirl of cultures in collision and transition; and the legacy nurtured within the now roofless red walls.

Pecos Timeline

C. 8000 BC–800 AD
    PaleoIndians, Hunter/Gatherers in Area
C. 800 AD–1300 AD
    Early Village Communities in Valley
C. 1300
    Great Pecos Pueblo Being Built
1540–1541
    Coronado's Expedition at Pecos
1598
    Spanish Colonization Begins in New Mexico
1619
    Spanish Mission Begins at Pecos
1625
    Father Andrés Juárez' Huge Church Completed
1680
    Pueblo Revolt Drove Out Spanish Settlers
1692
    Spaniards Returned Under Don Diego de Vargas
1717
    The Last Mission Church Completed
1760
    Bishop Tamarón's Visit
1776
    Father Domínguez' Inspection Tour

1786
> Marauding Comanches Pacified by Governor Juan de Anza

1790
> Spanish Settlers Moving Into Pecos Valley

1821
> Mexico Gained Independence from Spain
> Santa Fe Trail from Missouri Opened

1838
> Few Remaining Pecos Indians Migrated to Jemez Pueblo

1846
> American Troops Annexed New Mexico

1848
> Treaty of Guadalupe Hidalgo Ended Mexican War

1862
> Civil War Battle of Glorieta Pass

1880
> Railroad Completed Through Pecos Valley
> Archaeologist Adolph Bandelier Examined Pecos Ruins

1912
> New Mexico Gained Statehood

1915
> A.V. Kidder and J. Nusbaum began Archaeological Work at Pecos

1934
> Pecos State Monument Established

1965
> Pecos Created a National Monument
> Further Excavations of Church and Convento

1984
> E. E. Fogelson Visitor Center Dedicated

1990
> Pecos Elevated to National Historical Park

1999
> Repatriation of Ancient Burials

Fray Luis

The first missionary to Pecos came with Coronado in 1540. He was Fray Luis de Úbeda, an old Franciscan lay brother. With Coronado's huge expedition, he walked the rugged trails through mountain passes and deserts. He wondered at the different peoples they encountered and fretted at the abuses some of the soldiers inflicted upon them. He helped raise crosses in pueblo plazas and tended the sick and injured members of the expedition. He saw the buffalo out on the great grasslands, sat in on some of the parleys between Spanish and Indian leaders, tried to bring comfort and spiritual strength to those in need—and he prayed constantly. He was a simple soul who never complained and was much respected by the soldiers for his poverty and devotion.

The Pecos people initially welcomed Coronado with his army of perhaps fifteen hundred soldiers, Mexican Indian allies, and the slaves who tended to the livestock and did the work of the camp. The pueblo was a trading center and its people were used to many kinds of visitors. They were amazed at the horses (did they eat children?), their shining armor, the sharp swords, the noisy guns and the fierce war-dogs, the striped tents and copper kettles. They were fascinated with the cattle, sheep, goats, pigs and chickens that fed the army on the march, and with the pale-skinned men with hairy faces. They marveled at the strange ceremonies that were very imperfectly interpreted as trumpets blared and drums thundered and incomprehensible speeches were delivered, calling them to allegiance to a far-off, unknown king and faith. When gray-robed priests erected a huge cross in the plaza and the soldiers themselves bowed down to it, some of the Pecos men politely climbed up to adorn it with flowers and feathers. The Spaniards considered this a very good sign.

The Spaniards in their turn were delighted with this, "the biggest and most prosperous pueblo we have encountered," which had received them in friendship.

But soon relationships soured. Demanding information about a rumored—but non-existent—gold bracelet, the Spaniards made prisoners of two of the leading pueblo men, abusing and chaining them "like dogs."

The Pecos sent the invaders on a wild goose chase far out on the plains in hopes they would get lost and starve. When Coronado realized this plot against them, he had their guide, *El Turco*, garroted, and his army returned to the pueblo with blood in its eye. The Pecos people wavered, sometimes fighting, sometimes expressing friendship, sometimes seeking peace. Eventually, the situation stabilized and the Spaniards departed and made their way back to Mexico (New Spain, as it was then called).

But not Fray Luis. He was an old man and probably dreaded the long hike across the vast distances. Perhaps he felt particularly called to minister to the Pecos. All he asked was the company of a young slave boy named Cristóbal and perhaps a few sheep. He had his chisel and adze and planned to make crosses to give to receptive people, and to baptize dying children so their souls would fly to heaven. He expected that Cristóbal would quickly learn the Pecos language and become his interpreter and helper. The Pecos people promised to look after them.

The last the Spaniards saw of Fray Luis was when some soldiers were delivering the requested sheep. The Pecos were escorting the old man to visit another pueblo, and he expressed concern that they might kill him. (Another priest also stayed behind, venturing out into the plains where prospective Indian hosts soon murdered him.)

Perhaps the Pecos did kill Fray Luis. But an old tradition tells that the Pecos people gave him a small room, and every day the women brought him tortillas and *atole*—as they had promised. The old men, on the other hand, still rankling from Spanish abuses, ignored him, scowling at his greetings of "May God convert you." In spite of their great ambivalence, their fear and fascination about the Spanish invaders, they may have cared for him until he died.

Which possibility is true? Quick death or tolerant acceptance? We'll never know. But I lean toward the latter. The Pecos were described as basically kind and hospitable people, used to many diverse strangers, absorbing many into their midst. In addition, the old man might have represented something else: a useful hostage, perhaps, or a bargaining chip should the Spanish armies return, or a source of information about the ways of those strange people.

What of the sheep? Gone without a trace.

As for Cristóbal, the little slave boy? Presumably he was a Mexican Indian, raised in a *convento* or in a Spanish Christian family. If he lived, he may have learned the Pecos language as quickly as anticipated and become a good helper to Fray Luis. What did he tell the Pecos people about the Spanish people, about his life among them, about his travels and the things he had seen along the way, and about the faith of this strange man he cared for? The Pecos may have valued him as a source of information about the strangers to the south, as a possible emissary, or as a key interpreter should the Spaniards return. Again we don't know. Was he absorbed into the pueblo after Fray Luis died? Did he escape and make his way back to Mexico bringing many insights about the Pecos people? Was he killed, or did he soon die of disease or abuse?

Cristóbal, like Fray Luis and the sheep, have disappeared from the records—but not from the imagination. Apparently, they left "no impression at all." But I wonder. Did their benign presence perhaps soften up the Pecos people in some subtle ways for later incursions of missionaries and the Spanish settlers? We don't know.

Cicuye

✝

Who were the people of Cicuye encountered by the Spanish explorers in the 1500s?

They were traders, farmers, warriors, hunters. They were toolmakers, weavers, skilled craftsmen. They were

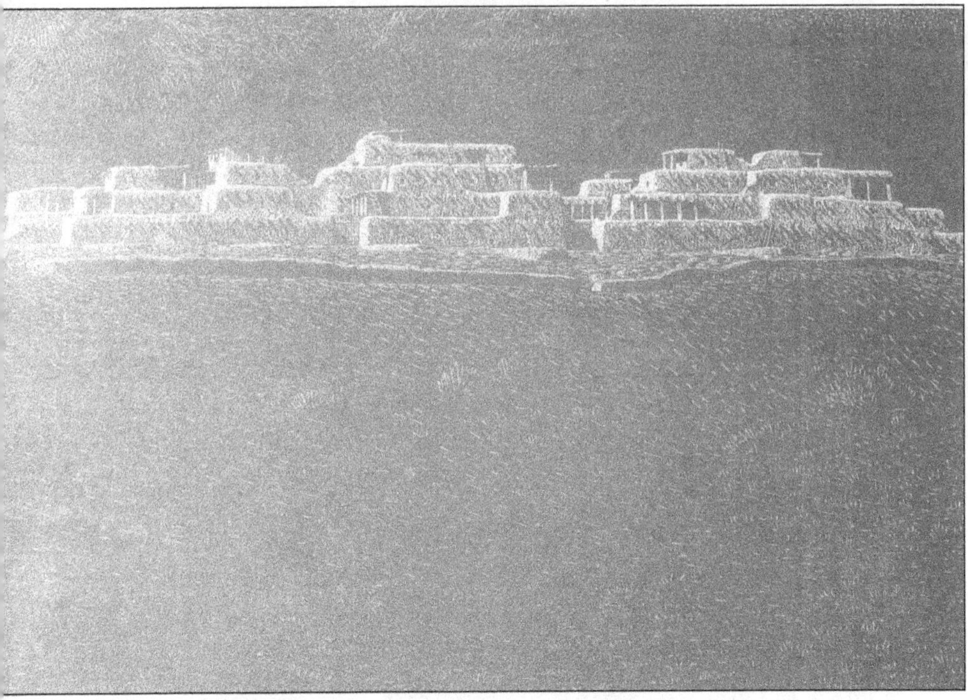

Pecos (Cicuye) Pueblo as described by early Spanish explorers.

priests, politicians, scalawags, witches, musicians with drums and flutes, and singers with deep, harmonious voices. They observed the heavens and surroundings for information, organized the rich ceremonial life of the people, and endeavored to keep the world in balance and the spirits in harmony.

Hillocks and humps reveal where the great Pecos Pueblo once stood.

The women were builders, keepers of home and hearth. They processed the crops the men harvested; gathered wild roots, berries, plants, piñon nuts, herbs; and cooked and cleaned as women do almost everywhere. They bore the babies and tended the children, cared for the old folks and ill. They gathered firewood, carried water, made baskets and pots and household utensils. They scraped and tanned hides and turned them into clothing and coverings. They were sharp traders and hospitable to strangers. They lived with their mothers and grandmothers in extended matrilineal families, inviting their men to join them — or leave.

Everybody worked, from dawn to dark, for life was hard — as it was almost everywhere. Children and old folks had their tasks according to their abilities, as soon and as long as they were able. Slaves and immigrants from other tribes were welcome helpers, incorporated into the community.

But life was also rich, with ceremonies, visitors, laughter, games, gambling, music and storytelling. It was spiced with gossip, flirtations, feuds, conflicts, scandals, fights, dissentions. There were joy and grief, endurance in times of trouble, love of family and friends, satisfaction at full storerooms and successful hunts, celebrations honoring special events, seasonal dances throughout the year, sharing of labor and delights and concerns and fears — all seasoning the dailiness of the lifelong chores.

The pueblo was an animated beehive of activity, a close-knit community in spite of frequent dissentions and internal tensions. The worst punishment for an offender was banishment.

As traders, some of the men traveled far, encountering unfamiliar people, places, customs, goods. At the great trade fairs at the pueblo, they welcomed strangers of many kinds who brought products from everywhere. Abalone shells from the Pacific, parrots from Mexico, oyster shells from the Mississippi, flint from Michigan, tools and salt and buffalo meat and foodstuffs, medicines, and charms and toys and jewelry — and captives — and much more were traded on the field below the pueblo. Some items came directly from distant places, others were passed along from tribe to tribe along the way.

And being traders, the Cicuye people weren't afraid of outsiders, were interested in new ideas, schemed to get "the best deal" possible. When Coronado was reported to have arrived at far-off Zuni, the Cicuye sent emissaries to meet the Spanish invaders and try to become allies instead of victims. They were considered friendly and compassionate people, kind hosts, generous to those in need — but also fierce, implacable enemies.

But the innovative spirit of traders often conflicted with the conservativism of the farmers, though most people were some of both. Openness to the new versus reliance on the traditional often created tensions and feuding factions in the not-so-cohesive community.

As farmers, they staggered the planting of their small garden plots of corn-beans-squash along the nearby creek and the more distant river so that the heavy frosts that come to this high country both early and late would not destroy everything. Digging sticks, stone or bone hoes (like buffalo shoulder blades) were the primary tools. In some places irrigation ditches were made, but often an occasional pot of water from the stream was sufficient to insure healthy plants near the water sources. Insects, birds, rabbits, deer and bears had to be fended off as the plants grew, the choking weeds removed, and prayers had to be offered at each stage of the growth. They also raised some gourds for many purposes, melons, and a form of tobacco. At harvest the men carried the crops to the pueblo, where the women took charge of preparation and preservation.

When the first Spanish visitors investigated, they estimated that enough food was stored away to feed the pueblo and visitors for three years.

They hunted deer, elk, bear, rabbit, buffalo, and other animals with arrows, spears, nets, snares, and clubs, with an intimate knowledge of the terrain and the habits of their prey. And the spirits of the animals had to be propitiated with offerings and ceremonies. In spite of the abundance of such animals, the large population at the pueblo depended greatly on the dried buffalo meat acquired from the Plains Indians who came to trade.

As weavers, they created mats, baskets, sandals, and cordage from the vegetation in the area. Vast amounts of cotton were traded from pueblos farther south: the men wove it into sacred dance kilts and sashes, blankets that were often painted with intricate designs, and fabric from which the women created garments. The women wove warm blankets of feathers from turkeys, the only domesticated creatures that the people raised besides dogs.

Their tools of stone, bone and wood were efficient and easy to replace. Obsidian knives can cut as cleanly as steel ones, and their bows and arrows were more effective for hunting and fighting than the firearms available for years to come. They made miles of cordage, from yucca fibers, sinews, rawhide and cotton, which they used for everything: fine sewing, weaving, sturdy sandals, carrying straps for burdens, tough bow strings—and so much more. Implements for every phase of domestic, economic and ceremonial life were created in abundance, from heavy grinding stones to sharp-pointed awls, from storage jars to sturdy ladders, from hoes to flutes, from *kachinas* to cradles.

Ornaments proliferated, made from stone and bone, shells, claws and teeth of large animals, feathers and fur, pottery shards and turquoise. They made pipes of clay, for smoking the local tobacco was both ceremonial and recreational. Whistles, small figurines, little animals and toys were created from clay and other materials. Gambling pieces were devised for various games. Many things were profusely decorated with painted or incised designs, for beauty went along with utility. The patience needed to drill tiny holes in tiny beads by the hundreds boggles the mind.

The women built and tended the house blocks, their domain, and many families took pride in their work. Each extended family was allotted 15-20 rooms on all levels: storage rooms on the bottom entered from above by ladders, two or three layers of rooms above for living and sleeping and more storage, and some roof space for drying corn and keeping turkeys away from the dogs and cooling off in the hot summers.

The basic food was corn, which they prepared in many ways. Fresh ears were roasted or boiled. Ground into meal of different consistencies, it was added to stews, made into the popular drink called *atole*, baked on a hot stone as the thin *piki* bread or tortillas, cooked as a mushy porridge, or baked in the ashes in the form of cakes. The women spent hours every day at the grinding stones, sometimes set in groups of three for different consistencies. It was hard, tedious work, enlivened with gossip and jokes when several women worked together. Sometimes a boy with a flute would entertain them with music and song.

Beans, dried, in many varieties, were another major staple; while squash — also of many varieties — either fresh or dried, was an all-season vegetable. They seasoned their soups and stews with herbs from the countryside, added a pinch of the precious salt brought from salt lake beds to the south, and added whatever roots, wild onions, or other plants were available. Piñon nuts were a valuable source of protein and fat and kept indefinitely; berries and wild fruits could also be preserved. Meats — deer, elk, bear, rabbit, antelope, birds — were eaten fresh or dried as jerky, and depended on the luck of the hunters or successful trading with the people from the buffalo plains. Most years, there was plenty to eat and the storerooms held ample surplus to trade or give away. But some years severe drought caused near famine conditions.

The ceremonial life was rich and complex, based on keeping the people in harmony with the spirits of the earth. The men gathered in underground *kivas* to plan, prepare and practice for the seasonal dances and other rituals entailed. This was a major commitment, which involved most of the men for long periods of time, for every aspect of life was related to the spiritual world. There were special prayers and rituals at sunrise to greet the day, others included the scattering of sacred corn meal while planting corn, when greeting guests, after a successful hunt, when digging clay for pottery, when setting out or returning from a journey. There were rituals for marking sacred spaces, for worshiping at shrines scattered throughout the area, for honoring the ancestors who had gone on to the spirit world. The *kachinas*, representations of the particular spirits of earth and sky, were sacred images, brought out at dances and on special occasions. The priests, the holy men who watched the stars and communed with the spiritual world, controlled the life of the people, and their influence was all-pervasive and powerful. (Not much different from the European patterns of the 1500–1600s.)

Drought, disease, disaster and personal misfortunes occurred when the ceremonies were not performed properly and the gods were angry, allowing the bad spirits and witches to disrupt the desired harmony. (In Europe at this time, witches were feared and executed, and disasters were attributed to a vengeful God punishing his people for their sins. Not so very different.)

Dissention within the pueblo was discouraged as a disruption of the desired harmony under the leadership of the priests. But people being people, and the Cicuye, with their broad exposure to diverse customs beyond the confines of their village, being particularly independent and individualistic, sometimes had their own ideas. Internal factions often led to conflicts that did disrupt the harmony and erupted from time to time.

Pity the poor Stone Age primitives? No. Their lives, health and happiness were as rich as any others in the world at that time. They were sophisticated, well adapted to their environment, and a powerful presence throughout the region. And well able to deal with "outsiders."

And then came the Spanish invaders.

The Spanish Invaders

Thousands of them poured over the islands and continents of the New World. Men without women seeking adventure, new discoveries, riches, land, opportunities for a new life.

It was an amazing national outpouring. The Moors had finally been driven out of Spain. The country of feuding small kingdoms was now unified under the crown of Castile. Christian Catholicism was proclaimed the only true and permissible faith, and the "Catholic Kings," Ferdinand and Isabella, were ready for new adventures. In only fifty years, Spanish banners flew and Spanish horses trampled over the whole of what is now called Spanish America, from New Mexico to Patagonia. Theoretically, a lad who had sailed with Columbus in the 1490s could have ridden with Coronado in 1542. And in their wake, new cities rose, unimaginable riches were discovered, and a new civilization was planted on the roots of the old.

The Spaniards died by the thousands. They drowned in shipwrecks and storms at sea. Tropical fevers, harsh climates, and failure to adapt to local conditions sapped their energies for survival. They starved when supplies ran low, got lost in vast distances. They joined expeditions that vanished and were never heard from again. Attacks from hostile warriors decimated them, and warring factions of *conquistadores* slaughtered each other with impunity. A taxi driver in Malaga, Spain, lamented to me, "We sent you the best we had, our young men. And now you call us beasts..."

They found sophisticated civilizations and great cities that rivaled those they knew in Europe. Brown-skinned people, unimaginable masses of them, organized, skilled, fierce fighters, willing workers thronged the land. Gold and silver in quantities that could fund European wars and unbalance economies brought yearned for riches. Foods strange to them eventually became worldwide staples: corn, the life-giving grain that nourishes both people and livestock; potatoes and beans in many varieties that keep hunger at bay; tomatoes, chiles and chocolate to pep up the palate; turkeys, sweet potatoes, squashes that grace Thanksgiving tables; medicinal plants, rubber, tobacco, chewing gum; and so much more.

The Spaniards brought to the New World what they knew. Horses, fearsome creatures that frightened the Indians at first. Swords of fine Toledo steel. Armor that repelled hostile arrows. Guns, crossbows and other weapons. Cattle for meat and hides. Sheep for wool and Spanish looms to weave it into cloth. Pigs that proliferated and fed armies on the march. Chickens. Wheat and the clay ovens for making bread. Sugar, rice and Spanish wines. Fruit trees of many varieties. Tools, hammers, chisels, knives, needles. Wheels, wagons, roads. Mills for grinding grain. Paper, ink and voluminous reports in multiple copies. The Catholic Christianity of the Middle Ages, the only allowed faith, compelled and enforced by the dreaded Inquisition. A medieval political system subservient to the king in the form of his stand-in, the viceroy. A feudal land tenure with tenants, usually native residents, owing tribute and labor to the landowner. Colorful fabrics, fine pottery. Musical instruments, paintings and statues. Big bronze bells. Architecture in styles never before seen in the New World. And more... and European diseases for which the native people had no immunity and which, according to some estimates, killed off ninety percent of the populations.

The *conquistadores,* though few in numbers, were able to subdue much larger native armies: their horses, attack dogs, steel weapons, and discipline overcame with little difficulty the arrows, spears, and obsidian-studded war clubs of their adversaries; and the carnage was horrific. But more important were their allies from other native communities that were often at war with each other. The invaders could easily intimidate more peaceful people with show of force and their long, incomprehensible speeches and ceremonies. Many native communities were well disciplined and used to taking orders from their rulers; so the change of overlords was not such a difficult transition.

As the Spanish immigrants settled in, they used the people in their areas in many ways. Some as slaves in brutal, backbreaking labor in the mines; others in construction of new Spanish communities; many as laborers on farms and factories, as porters and camp helpers on expeditions, as artisans and domestic servants.

Of course, men without women used and abused the native women. Their offspring launched the *mestizo* race, in an incredible variety of colors and castes. Many of these liaisons became permanent, caring relationships whose children were loved, educated, and became leading citizens of the next generations.

The viceroys, based in Mexico City and later also in Lima, had an almost impossible task. They had to administer, in the name of the king, the huge territories on both continents, from New Mexico to Patagonia, with all the crises and opportunities and prickly Spaniards involved. They were responsible to the Council of the Indies in Seville, and oversaw all the governors and functionaries that carried out the work of the government. Each of them, at the end of their term, produced a report that could be challenged and often led to trial.

For instance, Juan de Oñate who brought the first settlers to New Mexico was accused of cruelty and mismanagement, stood trial, and was shipped back to Spain. Coronado, on the other hand, though similarly accused, was acquitted and retired peacefully to his ranch.

Many of the men involved were honorable and effective; others were not and only wanted to fill their pockets. But the system was ripe for corruption and often abused.

Churches sprang up everywhere, splendid big ones in the cities and smaller missions elsewhere—many still in use. The Christianization and Hispanicization of the native people were major aspects of the colonial agenda. Missioners often used harsh methods to win converts, destroying sacred objects and introducing severe punishments to ensure compliance with this new, puzzling religion, which of course caused much resentment. Other priests cared for their people in different ways, treating them with respect, and teaching with patience and drama the basics of the new faith. Some of them became the first ethnologists, recording glossaries of the native languages, descriptions of their lifeways and beliefs, and saving from destructive fires some of the bark-paper picture books of the native heritage. And the missioners, in varying alliances, often protected their charges from abuses by the civil authorities and settlers.

But who were these people of the New World? How should the Spaniards relate to them? Were they mere beasts, primitives that could be enslaved, brutalized, and worked to death for Spanish profits? Or were they children of God, with souls to be saved, able to learn, to become productive contributors to the Spanish Empire? Were they to be used, abused, enslaved, or protected, cherished, respected—to what extent and in what proportions?

The debate raged for decades in Spain and throughout its colonies. Bartolomé de las Casas, a Dominican priest and later a bishop, led the movement for reform. Appalled at the frequent abuses by Spaniards who enslaved and exterminated native people, he wrote scathing letters to authorities in Spain demanding change. He made countless trips across the Atlantic to advocate in person and gather supporters. Peaceful persuasion rather than violent conquest, humane treatment rather than brutal enslavement, respect and consideration rather than scorn for these people, Children of God. He put his ideas into practice in his ministries; and they worked, incurring the wrath of the powerful "exploiters" who needed passive workers for their enterprises.

As a result of his influence, the Spanish government promulgated a series of laws, *Las Nuevas Leyes de las Indias*, demanding respect and fair treatment for the native people, whether slave or free. Over time, the laws expanded to several volumes, outlining every possible situation. Sometimes the laws were upheld, sometimes rejected by the colonists. Abuses continued, but so did the impetus for justice and the law. Whether recognized or not, *Las Leyes* was an unprecedented document, unknown in any other colonial nation.

In the early 1600s, Mexico City was a thriving, sophisticated metropolis. The former Aztec capital, Tenochtitlan, had been rebuilt by native workmen directed by Spanish engineers. The huge markets were bustling, with foodstuffs brought in from the countryside in enormous flat-bottomed canoes along the canals, in wagons trundled along the remains of the ancient causeways, slung on the backs of barefoot porters trotting along the dusty tracks. Goods from everywhere came through the custom houses and commercial centers: gold and silver bars from the mines of Guanajuato to the north and Potosi from Peru; silks, spices and porcelain from the orient; tools, fashions, delicacies, dignitaries from Spain; and so much more. Workshops hummed along the streets where native workers wove textiles, hammered copper pots, painted elegant pottery, made sturdy wooden furniture, created toys, musical instruments, art objects to delight the eyes, statues and paintings for churches and chapels. Government officials and their scribes wrote up masses of official documents in multiple copies. Festivals, Saints' Days, arrivals and departures, funerals, executions, and celebrations of one thing or another filled the plazas with gayety, color, and drama. And the social life of the wealthy extravagantly cast care to the winds.

Far to the north, New Mexico, *Las Provincias Internas*, was a rough frontier area where Spanish settlers and their Indian servants struggled for survival. The huge supply wagons that set out every three years from Mexico City needed six months to reach Santa Fe, the main town and center of government. It was a small community of low adobe buildings, with its farms and ranches spreading out along the creeks and watercourses. Huge tracts of land—*encomiendas*—had been granted in the name of the king to favored Spaniards who demanded tribute (goods) and labor from the pueblo people living within their boundaries. Traditional pueblo lands were protected by the missions assigned to their communities and the missions also required tribute and labor from their charges.

New Mexico was a poor province, marginally productive, providing only a sparse living for all its inhabitants. Poor in mineral wealth and resources, it was rich in its pueblo people. Pueblo farming villages were spread out along the Rio Grande watershed, each independent, speaking various languages and dialects, and often in conflict with each other. Christian missions for the saving of the souls and the hispanicization of the pueblo people became the rationale for the existence of the province. Theoretically, the civil government existed to support the missions, and the settlers were there to support both.

Franciscan missions were established in many of the larger pueblos where the missionaries directed the building of churches and taught as well as they could the rudiments of the faith. Some of them used harsh methods, trying to destroy the native religions to make way for the new. Others tried to work with the native leaders in the spirit of *Las Leyes,* to bring the people to Christianity in more effective ways.

But both the civil and clerical authorities required tribute and labor from the pueblos for their own survival—sometimes to excess. Though mission Indians were theoretically exempt from secular labor, the competition for their services was often intense and surged back and forth in varying patterns, affecting everybody. Official policies shifted from time to time, sometimes demanding a heavy fist, and sometimes consideration and justice. The two authorities, church and state, often worked together harmoniously, but sometimes were in open conflict regarding policies. Regardless, each missioner and government official applied the policies according to their own conscience and temperament.

One frequent stereotype pictures a solitary, sandal-clad priest, his blue robe flapping about his ankles, a broad-brimmed hat shielding him from the blistering sun, a staff in his hand, striding valiantly across the landscape to launch a new mission. We wonder at his courage and resourcefulness.

But this picture is misleading. The missions were not solitary affairs. They were highly organized and well supported endeavors supplied at intervals from the resources in Mexico. The bureaucracy, based at Santo Domingo Pueblo, was immense, authoritarian, and oversaw the work at each mission.

In 1680, the pueblos had had enough of Spanish control and joined together to throw the Spaniards out of their land. Twelve years later, the Spaniards returned, this time with a more relaxed relationship with the pueblo people, leading eventually to more cooperation than conflict.

But by that time, the official priorities were reversed. The civil government now took precedence over the missions. Protection of the Spanish settlements and pueblos from marauding Navajos, Utes, Comanches, Apaches, and from the incursions of French and English expeditions advancing across the eastern plains, became paramount. Strategically, New Mexico was now an essential buffer, shielding the great wealth of Central Mexico from European, and later American, encroachment.

The mission at Pecos was an active participant in all that happened.

The Mission Builder

When Father Andrés Juárez was assigned to the Pecos mission in 1621, he was already a battle-scarred veteran of ten years of New Mexico mission politics, well aware of the problems, possibilities, challenges, conflicts and great opportunities ahead of him.

His assignment, as was that for most missionaries in that early period, was immense. He was to:

Overcome the resistance of the people and build up their trust in the mission. His predecessor had smashed sacred objects, disrupted ceremonies, and denigrated the elders in his zeal to convert the "benighted heathen" to the true faith, which of course caused massive resentments;

Bring the people to Christianity, baptizing, confirming and teaching the elements of the faith, without violence or force, as mandated by the Laws of the Indies;

Conduct regular masses, liturgies, rosaries, confessions, festivals, and all the other ceremonies of Christian worship with all the drama and splendor available, and serve outlying settlements with the resources of the faith;

Teach the people the new skills brought by the

Hispanic settlers, to improve their way of life and make them productive citizens of the greater Spanish empire;

Make the mission economically self-supporting as much as possible and to provide appropriate tithes and tributes to the central mission treasury;

Defend the people in his care from abuses by secular authorities, from the wiles of the devil, from harassment by hostile outsiders, and from the horrors of hell after death;

Reach out beyond the Pecos valley to the Plains tribes that came there to trade; and

Complete the massive church and *convento* laid out by his predecessor.

This was enough of a task for any one person, even one with the energy and dedication of Father Andrés. This was not an unusual challenge for the intrepid early missionaries.

How did he do these things? Where did he start?

He learned the Towa language of the Pecos people so he could communicate directly instead of only through indifferent interpreters. As mandated by the Law of the Indies and his own humane temperament, he respected the elders and their ceremonies. He listened to them and adapted many of their practices to help teach Christian doctrines. And he started classes in practical Spanish for those who wanted to learn.

He brought in artisans and craftsmen from among the settlers to teach their skills: carpentry, shearing sheep and weaving wool (rather than the traditional cotton), baking bread, making cheese; animal husbandry and use of their products; cultivation of fruit trees, wheat, unfamiliar vegetables, tomatoes and chiles from Mexico. He brought into the mission flocks of sheep and goats, some cattle, pigs, chickens, horses and mules, and burros for lugging loads. Steel knives, hoes and axes were some of the useful tools introduced, as were wheeled carts and chimney pots to draw smoke out of interior rooms. As traders interested in new products and technologies, many Pecos people were drawn to the mission. Others resisted its blandishments.

The great church created by Fr. Andres Juarez, completed in 1625, was the pride of the New Mexico missions.

And the church. The Pecos people had never dreamed of such a structure. Ox teams borrowed from settlers hauled in tons of rock, earth and timbers. Loads of fill leveled the uneven bedrock of the ridge; the foundations were made sturdy and strong. Adobe bricks, a technique that had been brought to Spain from North Africa by the Moors many centuries earlier, was a new technology for the Indians. The bricks were shaped in wooden molds and dried in the sun—thousands of them. Built into the walls some 60 feet high, each of the estimated 300,000 bricks weighed

60 to 80 pounds. The scaffolding needed must have been immense. The roof was as wide as available logs dragged down from the mountains permitted. Covered with networks of close-fitting cedar poles, brush and layers of clay, a clerestory shedding light on the altar, the roof was impervious to the worst of weather. Plastered and whitewashed inside and out, it shone in the sun, as did the pueblo at the other end of the ridge. When the huge bronze bell was installed in one of the six towers, its sound bonged out over the valley, vying with the deep throbbing of the pueblo drums. People came from far and wide to see this magnificent structure, and Father Andrés made sure the Pecos people showed off their work with pride.

Walls sixty feet tall dwarfed the worshippers in procession. The church could hold all 2,000 members of the pueblo, and was visible for miles.

The two-story *convento* was also developing as space for multiple tasks: living quarters for the priest and his helpers, storerooms, classrooms, meeting rooms, guest rooms, workshops, stables, kitchen—whatever was needed at any given time. As the church was the ceremonial center, the *convento* was the working heart of the mission.

What happened in and around them?

The Catholic faith is full of drama and color. Processions with tall, shining crosses, pots of incense swinging on their chains and emitting fragrant smoke; colorful vestments, banners blowing in the breeze. Trumpets and deep-voiced bells that draw people in to join in whatever is happening. Religious plays and pageants to bring "alive" far-off events, from Christmas and Easter to saints' days. Replays of dramatic "battles" in which noble Christians defeat and convert infidel Moors. Music of many kinds, from psalms and hymns to folk canticles honoring the Virgin, and carols celebrating the birth of her Son. The mass itself, with the people standing and kneeling on command, shouting the liturgical refrains as directed by the *fiscales*, the priest's helpers and catechists. The priest in his vestments holding high the Bread of Life, and elevated in the pulpit preaching with authority his baffling theological message, often made more baffling by inept interpreters. The interior of the church aglow with candles, using precious wax for special occasions or ordinary tallow for everyday use. Colorful paintings and statues of saints, some brought by wagon from Mexico, others created locally by pueblo people like them, with paint on buffalo hide or elk skin, that brought a human dimension into the huge church. The altar shining with chalice, cross and candlesticks; the small pump organ (even in the 1600s in New Mexico) wheezing out melodies and accompanying the (hopefully) well-trained choir. Drama, excitement, mystery. There was much to attract, as well as repel, the people for whom it was intended.

And what youngster could resist the opportunity to ring the huge bell in the tower, sending its call far out over the countryside, or to blow blasts on the trumpet to celebrate joyous occasions, or to wear a special robe and carry a tall cross or lighted candle in a procession, or to sing with others in a choir making music to delight the ear, or portraying a Roman soldier or an angel or a wicked Moor in one of the pageants, or to ride a mission mule carrying a message for a distant pueblo?

And what adult would not be pleased with payment for mission work in the form of an ample meal of unfamiliar foods, a steel knife, a clutch of hens eggs, round loaves of wheat bread, a warm wool blanket for cold winter nights, a goat, or a peach tree to plant near the creek? If the spiritual message was fuzzy, the material incentives were strong.

Many people became nominal Christians, whether or not they understood the theology. Others resisted, in the correct belief that these things and new "gods" and ceremonies were upsetting the traditional way of life, and distorting relationships with the ancient spirits that had protected the people for hundreds of years. With food animals available, people were losing patience with the hunt and its rituals; new tools made the age-old stone ones obsolete; the mission ceremonies drew the young people away from the traditional spiritual practices of their people. Disaster was sure to come: the gods would be angry. Resistance to change defied the mission endeavors, as ancient divisions within the community festered. Patience, counseled the mission authorities: forced conversions are forbidden by the Laws of the Indies, and besides, they don't work. Use the proverbial carrot instead of the stick.

But the mission was not only about conversion and new Hispanicized lifeways. It was also about economic subsistence. Pueblo workers cultivated mission fields, tended mission flocks, worked in the carpentry shop, the weaving room, the tannery, the kitchen, in construction. They were porters and messengers and bell-ringers and artists. They contributed corn, beans, squash, piñon nuts, deerskins, cotton blankets, pottery vessels, and more for the mission storerooms. Much of the work produced was returned to the people in times of need or in repayment for service, and much was sent off in the great wagons to support the central mission establishment and to purchase in Mexico goods to be brought in with the triennial supply caravans.

Father Andrés oversaw everything that happened. He had help. Two or three *fiscales* assisted in teaching elements of the faith and reaching out to the local people. In the beginning, the *fiscales* were Christianized Mexican Indians, later native converts. He had interpreters, some excellent, others not so good, to help him communicate with the many kinds of people revolving around the mission. Craftspeople with special talents were enlisted from among the settlers to teach the Pecos their skills. The support of the central mission office headquartered at Santo Domingo Pueblo was essential.

And the supply wagons that trekked along the Camino Real from Mexico arrived every three years or so in the early years, later more often. Caravans of thirty-two huge, four-wheeled vehicles, each drawn by eight mules caparisoned with banners and bells, brought a huge variety of goods to the missions: tools and hardware; bells and plows; seeds and anvils; fabric for vestments, banners and altar cloths; new robes, sandals and hats for the priests; communion wine and beeswax for candles; paper and ink; hymnals and musical instruments; paintings and statues to adorn the churches; medicines and rosaries; olives and chocolate for the priests' tables; and much more to enhance the work of the mission and the comfort of the priest. Picture the excitement when one of the wagons drew up at the *convento* doorway, with the people gathered around to see the treasures unloaded.

The Laws of the Indies were very specific about use of the native people. Use, but not abuse. Respect and care for their needs. They should be rotated in their work for the mission so that the labor would not overburden anyone. Adequate time should be allowed for tending their own crops, families and ceremonies. The tithes demanded by the mission should never be excessive. Father Andrés tried to abide by these laws, respecting the needs of the workers, feeding them well from the mission kitchen, rewarding them however he could.

But he also had to deal with the outside world, protecting his people from exploitation as much as possible. The *encomienda* system was then in effect, giving area landowners rights to labor and tribute from the people on their lands. Theoretically, mission Indians were exempt, but this was not easy to enforce. Then there were the illegal slavers who, with or without official connivance, raided the plains tribes for captives to work on their ranches or to be sold to the mines in Mexico. Often, these captives were from trading partners, friends and allies of the Pecos. And the civil government sent wagons and soldiers periodically to collect tribute (taxes) from the pueblo people, regardless of the people's ability to supply the corn, piñon nuts, tanned hides, cotton blankets, and other material demanded. Father Andrés, like most of the other missionaries, was constantly protesting, protecting, advocating, fighting bruising battles with the secular authorities and would-be exploiters of the people in his care.

His days must have been extremely busy. He was responsible for everything that happened in and around the mission, and for setting the tone of his ministry. He had to train his helpers, oversee their work, check on the condition of the animals, of the crops, the crafts, the food, new construction, classes, supplies in the storerooms. He prepared the masses, the festivals, the liturgies, the music, and countless sermons and homilies.

He needed time for studying his breviary, for private prayer, for writing the voluminous reports required. He constantly reached out to the people, both pueblo and nearby settlers, learning more about their customs and internal politics and how he could help them most effectively. He conferred with their leaders, cared for the ill and troubled, tended to marriages, baptisms, confessions, burials, disputes — all the work of any parish minister. He welcomed steady streams of visitors, from other pueblos, from Santa Fe, from mission headquarters in Santo Domingo, from civil government representatives, from ranches, from plains tribes. He traveled to Santo Domingo headquarters, to Santa Fe, to other pueblos and Hispanic settlements on official business, and sometimes to the plains to visit trading partners of the Pecos on their home turf. (One story speculates how he could have refused the gift of a chief's daughter for the night, a great honor, without giving offense.) It was a huge amount of work, requiring stamina and commitment, and typical of the missionary labor of that era. No vacations. I wonder how he recharged his depleted batteries.

Father Andrés served at Pecos for thirteen years, much longer than any of the other priests who worked there. Suddenly he disappeared. Why? We can only speculate. Simple burnout? Some conflict within the pueblo he couldn't cope with? Problems or jealously within the mission establishment? Whatever, he reappeared later as the priest at Nambe Pueblo. But his major work had been at Pecos.

I have probably over-idealized Father Andrés beyond all reason. But his accomplishments speak for themselves, and they were typical of the work of effective missionaries throughout the Spanish empire in the New World. His legacy at Pecos lasted for generations. The pro-Christian, pro-Spanish bias of many of the Pecos people were important factors in the tumultuous years to come.

When you visit the Park, go into the ruins of the venerable churches. Be awed at the dimensions of the foundations of the first great mission church. Stand on the location of the high altar at the west end, feel the energies of that early mission vibrating through your feet, and say a prayer in memory of Father Andrés.

May he rest in peace.

The People Divided

✝

In 1680, all hell broke loose. For the first time in history, the pueblos joined together to drive the Spaniards out of New Mexico. The uprising was bloody and destructive: some 21 Franciscan missionaries, more than 400 settlers, and uncounted numbers of native people, both Christianized and traditional, were slaughtered. By the time the Spaniards returned twelve years later, the pueblo alliance had broken apart and the Spaniards, under Governor Don Diego de Vargas, were able to resume control

The reasons for the uprising were many. For eighty years, Spain had steadily increased its stranglehold over the people and the resources of the area. As government and mission policies shifted, demands for tribute and labor intensified to the point of severe hardships for the pueblos. Restrictions became ever more oppressive: they forbade ceremonies; destroyed sacred objects; jailed holy men; disparaged traditional languages, clothing, and customs; threatened to eradicate every vestige of what held the pueblos together as people. It didn't matter that severe drought had brought the people to the brink of starvation.

A particular leader, a charismatic holy man, Popé, raised the battle cry and roused the pueblos to action.

But it wasn't as simple as "bad Spaniards" versus "good Indians." Over the course of the years, some of the royal administrators, the land-grant holders and missionaries had been honest and capable men. Others had not. Some of the Indians were passive victims of oppression; others became skilled manipulators, learning how to use the systems to their advantage. For many, the missions brought protection from abuse and welcome new objects to enhance their lives, though at the expense of traditional lifeways and a goal of harmony with the spirits of the earth.

And almost every pueblo community was divided into pro- and anti-Spanish factions.

This was the situation at Pecos. Though many of the people supported the uprising, others did not. The missionaries over the past years must have done their work well. When runners brought news to the pueblo of the imminent uprising, the Pecos leaders alerted their priest, Fray Fernando de Velasco who warned the Spanish authorities. Popé changed the starting day for the revolt. Some of the mission Indians, hoping to save the respected veteran Padre Velasco, rushed him off to presumed safety at nearby Galisteo. But within sight of their destination they were overtaken by hostiles who killed the good padre and his escort. Back at Pecos, the young lay brother assigned to the mission was murdered, as were some Spanish women and children staying there while their husbands were away. The huge church was burned and demolished, its holy objects smashed, desecrated, destroyed.

Yet Popé, the brilliant instigator of the revolt, didn't last long. He became overbearing, dictatorial, demanding that the pueblo people reject everything the Spaniards had brought. Chop down the orchards. Trample the wheat fields. Kill the horses, mules, cattle, sheep, pigs and chickens so useful for food and work. Abandon the steel knives and the tools and skills they had acquired. Dissolve all Christian marriages, scrub off the waters of baptism, forget any Spanish they had learned. Revert to life as it had been lived a hundred years earlier, and then the gods would once more smile on the people.

This was too much. Most people had become accustomed to the conveniences and pleasures the Spaniards had brought and had no intention of abandoning them. Many resisted Popé and his demands, and communities were seriously divided. Within a year, Popé had been deposed and the fragile pueblo alliance had crumbled. As the drought continued and hostile tribes threatened on all sides, some people began to think that the Spaniards hadn't been so bad after all. In spite of considerable resistance to the idea, delegations traveled to El Paso to invite the colonists to return. The peaceful resettlement originally anticipated was not so peaceful. Quelling native resistance was in some pueblos a bloody affair.

When Governor Don Diego de Vargas brought soldiers and settlers back to New Mexico, many of the Pecos became valued allies. It may have been for strategic reasons, in self-interest, in genuine friendship, or all of these possibilities. Pecos warriors helped the Spanish troops recapture Santa Fe and punish rebellion ringleaders. They fought alongside the soldiers to subdue pueblos that continued to resist.

The Pecos governor, Juan Ye, became a trusted friend of Vargas, and was killed on a peace mission to Taos. Another Pecos governor, hoping to curry favor with Vargas, treacherously murdered several leaders of the Pecos opposition, in a sacred *kiva*, no less.

Governor Vargas rode with the Franciscan missionaries when they returned to the pueblo. He stood as godfather for many of the native people baptized at that time, sealing a spiritual and material relationship between their communities that endured for years.

But the divisions within the pueblo were deep. Many people left in fear of Spanish retaliations or of the incessant discord of a community in conflict. They scattered, their descendants becoming absorbed into other communities, from the plains to the western deserts. Pity the poor moderate folks in the middle who leaned to neither extreme.

Yet loyalty to the mission continued. Soon after the Spaniards returned, young Father Diego de Zeinos was assigned to Pecos. He erected a makeshift temporary church in the ruins of the destroyed one, revived the dramatic liturgies and repaired the damaged *convento*. He resumed the teaching of the faith and the tasks of the mission with whatever resources he could scrounge up. He obviously cared for the people, and *liked* them, even learning their difficult language. The people in turn liked him.

Then a tragic accident occurred. Someone had left a gun in the *convento*. Father Zeinos picked it up to look at it and—the familiar story— unaware that it was loaded, he accidentally discharged it. The shot killed one of his Indian helpers. The Indians knew it was an accident and did not blame the remorseful father. But the mission authorities whisked him away, fearful of repercussions. Delegations of Pecos leaders followed to appeal to the governor in Santa Fe and the Franciscan *custos* at mission headquarters at Santo Domingo, and then traveled down the Camino Real, requesting from all authorities the return of their vanished priest. To no avail. But what an impressive sign of devotion to their hapless Zeinos these efforts displayed.

Many historians consider the Pueblo Revolt the most significant event in New Mexico history. The success of the uprising taught the Spaniards respect for the native people. After the return of the colonists, many of the earlier abusive systems were abandoned, though a certain degree of exploitation continued in spite of new legal safeguards. Gradually, the pueblo people and Hispanic settlers came to see each other as neighbors, allies and friends, working together trying to survive in this harsh land.

The political focus had also changed. Because of French and English incursions into the Mississippi basin, the Spanish government now considered the Internal Provinces of New Mexico a buffer area, protecting the riches of central Mexico from traditional European enemies. Though the missions were still supported, they and the salvation of Indian souls were no longer the principal motive for the colonial effort. And Pecos, on the pass between the Rio Grande and the Great Plains, was in a strategic location and should be preserved as an additional buffer against hostile incursions.

A statue of Popé, as leader of this successful indigenous revolt against exploitative conquerors, has been created by Cliff Fragua of Jemez Pueblo. It represents New Mexico in the rotunda of the capitol in Washington.

Renewal and Decline

Frater Carolus. Brother Charles. The name was carved on a beam facing the nave of the new church finished in 1717. This would have been Carlos Jose Delgado, the only Carlos among the many priests who served the Pecos mission.

One of a bewildering variety of short-term priests at Pecos, he was only there a year. During the 21 years between him and Diego de Zeinos in 1695, the names of 16 others are listed. Yet in spite of the many different men in charge, the new church had somehow arisen from the ruins of the old, replacing the temporary chapel erected by Father Zeinos between the *convento* and the still-standing wall of the ruined church. From all accounts, it was beautiful, smaller than Father Andrés' earlier structure, nestled within the foundations on top of the rubble. The remains are still impressive.

Apparently Frater Carolus was a dynamic, energetic missionary who spent forty years serving the native people of New Mexico, reaching out to the Hopi and Navajo, among others. A page of his writing shows remarkably clear and confident script and delightful drawings of strawberries. (Did he miss them, yearn for them, grow them in the mission garden?) He was credited with finishing construction of the church, but how much remained to be done when he came along? Was he the inspiring construction boss after years of indifferent stop-and-go chaos? Did he preside over an elaborate dedication ceremony that gave the Pecos people pride in their accomplishment? Was he delighted or vain enough with the results to autograph the beam himself, or was it carved there by an admirer without his knowledge? And why did he serve so briefly at Pecos? Many questions, few answers.

The "new church," completed in 1717.

Throughout the whole 18th century, priests came and went in rapid succession, with 61 named on Dr. Kessell's list. One stayed as long as eight years, many for only a few months. Some returned for several tours of duty, many were part-timers serving several missions at the same time. At times, there was nobody there at all. Most of them were probably caring and capable men, though little was said about them in the brief notations listed. But there seemed to be a discouraging number of dysfunctional ones ... "accused of soliciting sex in the confessional" ... "charged with abusing the Indians" ... "old and ill" ... "notorious drunkard" ... "sicker than all the others."

The rear of the "new" church stands where the front of the "old" one stood. The directions were reversed because violence during the Pueblo Revolt had desecrated the original sanctuary, making it inappropriate for sacred activities.

Why was there such a revolving door at Pecos? It may have been mission policy because of the constant shortage of priests, or it may have been personal preference, or maybe something of each. Pecos was far out on the eastern frontier exposed to attacks by Comanches, Apaches, Utes and other hostile tribes. It was a good day's ride from the comforts and relative safety of Santa Fe. It was probably isolated and lonely, a hardship post. But so were many of the other missions. The Pecos people were surely no more difficult to work with than those of other pueblos, and better than some.

Whatever the reasons, the results were the same. The priests had scant time to learn the language or develop trusting relationships with the people under their care. The pueblos spoke many different languages—Towa, Tewa, Tiwa, Keres, Piro among them—and when a priest finally began to learn to communicate with his assigned people, he was frequently transferred to another pueblo where he had to start all over. (I know some bureaucracies nowadays that work like that.) Interpreters, sometimes deliberately and sometimes in ignorance, often caused more confusion than clarification. Though the priests were supposed to teach the Indians Spanish and were provided with books and readers to help the process, visiting bishops complained that the Pecos Spanish was unintelligible. (A personal observation: pueblo languages, including the Towa of the Pecos, are filled with strange sounds like hiccups, coughs, jerky pauses. I expect such speech patterns carried over, making it hard for outsiders to understand their Spanish even when it was reasonably accurate. And it's an ancient ploy to play dumb in front of mistrusted authorities.)

Under these circumstances, the *fiscales*, the Indian catechists and mission helpers, were essential intermediaries between mission and pueblo. They reached out to the people, instructed the priest, taught the children, provided rosary and prayer services, led the liturgies of the mass, and generally kept the mission going whether the priest was absent or present. They probably bullied the less confident ones and protected the people from the incompetent ones, and were influential individuals the priests had to reckon with. (Something like school secretaries now.) I don't think they get the credit they deserve in any of the accounts I have read.

Understandably, visiting clerics complained that the Pecos people, though they went to mass regularly, observed the rituals more-or-less, followed the responses of the mass as led by the *fiscales* and sang beautifully, knew little of the basics of the faith and often had not abandoned their own traditions. Priests, rather than the context, were blamed when the people seemed reluctant and resistant. Not fair.

The Pecos people had troubles enough of their own. Diseases, such as smallpox, measles, flu, swept through the pueblo, killing many. The Comanches and other hostile tribes raided. Droughts destroyed the crops. Taxes and tithes and labor were still demanded of them in spite of the protection of the law. Inner dissention within the pueblo created tensions and many people up and left. The population was dwindling, slowly, inexorably, depressingly. Mission and government policies kept changing, sometimes denigrating religious rituals, ancient customs, language and traditional clothing, and sometimes accommodating them. Some of their leaders were given fine horses and Spanish clothing and gear, a cause for frequent jealousy, and many looked to outsiders rather than their elders to resolve disputes. And the once helpful mission priests were distant, unknown, mistrusted.

While mission influence dwindled, that of the civil government increased. *Casas Reales* or *Casas de Comunidad* were constructed just west of the *convento*. This was a building, or a cluster of them, where government officials conducted their business. There was a lot of business concerning the Indians. Official notices were posted on the doors; government representatives came and went; official guests, bureaucrats and soldiers lodged there for long or short times; travelers could find food and shelter. There were taxes and labor and trade to see to. Warriors were recruited to join military expeditions. Conflicts among the Pecos people and with outsiders from other pueblos or the Spanish settlers were dealt with, generally fairly, by civil authorities. And since these authorities were relatively stable and served the area for years in contrast to the constantly changing priests, the people began to trust them more than the missionaries.

Naturally, the missions and the civil authorities were in constant conflict, each charging the other with excessive exploitation of the Indians and various forms of mistreatment. There must be many stories about how these conflicts played out and the different characters involved. But even the *Casas Reales*, site of much drama and excitement at Pecos, has been obliterated and seldom features in the interpretive comments of the Park rangers.

Yet in many ways, the pueblo thrived. The great trade fairs were still held in the field below the pueblo walls, times of official peace among all comers. Plains and Pueblos, Spaniards and Athabascans, fierce enemies during much of the year, gathered to exchange hides, meat, corn, pottery, turquoise, flint, cotton and wool blankets, horses, moccasins, bone tools, jewelry, steel knives, saddles and bridles, sugar and salt, wheaten cookies, chocolate, tanned deerskins, chickens, clothing and captives.

Nomadic Indians tribes raided each other, bringing children, women and sometimes men to trade. They found a ready market among the pueblos and settlers, who constantly needed more helping hands on their farms and ranches. Some of the youngsters brought up in Spanish households who had lost touch with their own heritage were called *genízaros* and became a special community of frontiersmen. Some were adopted as respected members of the Pecos community as they grew up, mingling with the other Pecos people and being noted as *genízaro* in the official church records as they were baptized, married and died.

Pecos fielded more fighters for the Spanish militia than most of the other pueblos. Military expeditions ranged far afield in search of French and English forces and Comanche bands. Pecos farmers tended their fields conscientiously, though drought and fear of Comanches sometimes limited their crops. Their horse herds were large, their cattle and sheep well fed. Many were fine carpenters, busy with projects throughout Northern New Mexico. They still supplied quantities of tanned deerskins and cotton blankets for trade or tribute. Their drums and flutes still echoed throughout the plaza. Dancers emerged from the *kivas*. The elders watched the stars from the high places. The girls carried handsome water jugs on their heads from the stream to their homes. The grinding stones scrunched the corn on the *metates*. The boys snared rabbits and small animals for dinner. The people laughed and sang and cried and manipulated the oppressors and told stories and lived their lives — and endured.

And the mission persisted in spite of its problems. Supply wagons arrived from Mexico periodically. They brought cases of chocolate to be stirred into a favorite drink. Sugar, fine tobacco, olive oil, paper, soap, tools, fabrics, books, musical instruments, wine, paintings for the church, crosses and bells, rosaries, shoes and hats for the priest, holy objects to distribute as gifts, and so much more. Were the priests able to protect these treasures from raids by the government officials? And when priests were scarce, how were these supplies utilized and by whom? Good questions.

Bishops came to visit rarely. But one of them left a memorable legacy.

The Two Bishops

In 1760, Bishop Tamarón visited Pecos Pueblo twice.

Most bishops were daunted by the long trek over vast wastelands between their base in Durango and the missions in the Northern Provinces. Many years elapsed between official visitations.

Bishop Pedro Tamarón y Romeral was an exception. He actually enjoyed travel, no matter how rough the road or rugged the journey. New sights and experiences delighted him. He was deeply concerned about the New Mexico missions, which had not had proper oversight for many years. Everywhere he went he was welcomed, for the mission friars needed his support against the abuses by civil authorities and a chance to air their concerns and accomplishments. He was also a caring and sympathetic guest.

As Bishop Tamarón traveled among the missions, he was accompanied by his black body servant and the *Father Custos*, the local mission supervisor, by a contingent of soldiers for protection against raiding Comanches, and by a number of helpers and hangers-on. They must have made quite a sight, with the bishop in his official traveling regalia, riding a mule, flanked on each side by his "man" and the blue-robed Father Custos.

At Pecos, the people welcomed him extravagantly. They showed off their horsemanship, their cleaned-up pueblo, their crafts and the many other things the bishop was pleased to see. And he listened to them. He confirmed and baptized many, conducted masses, preached eloquently, and brought the color, drama and authority of the church to this remote community. Pecos was not used to so much benign attention.

But the bishop was not pleased with the local mission. He admonished the local priest severely, which may not have been altogether fair because the priest had not been at Pecos very long. The bishop's concerns, however, applied to almost all of the pueblo missions.

His chief complaints were that the local priests had neither learned the pueblo languages nor made sure that the people under their care could speak and understand intelligible Spanish. They depended too much on the native *fiscales* who often intentionally or through ineptitude distorted messages in the process. As a result, the people were ill-informed about the faith, and although they followed the liturgies as required, most of them had little understanding of their significance. Confirmation and other rituals were, therefore, mere travesties, and as for confession, for the priest's ears alone, it was pointless and often ignored.

The previous years had been hard ones for the Pecos people. Comanche raids, smallpox and other diseases had devastated the community, and internal dissention had driven away many of their number. The once-proud pueblo of more than two thousand souls had been reduced to about three hundred fifty individuals. Priests had come and gone in rapid succession, some of them caring, some of them not, seldom staying more than a year. Of course, it was hard for them to learn the local language and foster enough confidence with the people for effective relationships. Conflict between the missions and civil government had added to the stress and confusion. And then there was drought.

Bishop Tamarón and his retinue left. But three months later, in

August, people watching from their rooftops saw a strange sight. A small procession of some soldiers and Indians were accompanying three men on mules. The central one was wearing a bishop's mitre on his head and robes such as the bishop had worn. He carried a crook in his hand. A huge shiny cross adorned his chest. On one side of him rode a large black man, on the other side a figure dressed in Franciscan blue. Excited, they shouted the news: "The bishop has returned."

When the procession entered the plaza, they realized what was happening. The "bishop" was Agustín Guichi, one of the leading men of the pueblo. He was a carpenter and one of the sacred clowns that enliven the religious dances with jokes and buffoonery. His two companions were also well known, one with his face painted black, the other mimicking the Father Custos. And the people quickly caught the spirit of the burlesque.

"Bishop" Agustín made his way between rows of kneeling women, drenching them with "holy water" and smacking their heads in blessing, to a hastily erected bower at one end of the plaza. First came confessions with people lining up to describe in loud voices the most outrageous sins they could think of, receiving absolution with smacks on the cheeks that sometimes staggered them. Later came confirmation, and eventually baptisms with the bishop holding babies upside down until they squealed and their mothers protested. For communion, he distributed bits of tortilla along with distorted liturgies and discordant music. Strange sermons with even stranger interpretations delighted the listeners. Agustín was a wonderful mimic and replicated the bishop's moves and mannerisms exactly. Everything brought forth howls of healing laughter, giggles and smiles that lasted for days.

For three days, this burlesque continued. At the command of the bishop, each afternoon and evening was devoted to feasting, games, social dancing, music, flirtations, fun and frivolity. What a respite from the concerns that had depressed the people for so long.

Eventually, the energy ran out, Bishop Agustín and his retinue departed, and the people returned to normal life. But their spirits had been restored, their courage returned, and they were ready to face the future.

There were some people, however, who were shocked and dismayed at the disrespect for the holy church and anticipated severe reprisals.

Soon afterwards Agustín went out to work in his cornfield. While he rested under a piñon tree, a bear emerged from the woods, attacked the dozing man and mauled him so severely that soon he died. But its behavior was very unusual for a bear, for it left after the unprecedented attack without even raiding the cornfield. The question lingered: was it really a bear? Before he died, Agustín is said to have confessed his great sin. It was considered that this was divine punishment for his elaborate satire of God's holy church.

When Bishop Tamarón (the real one) heard about it, he was delighted with the story. He wrote it up and had it printed and circulated widely. A true "lesson" for new Christians everywhere.

But for me, anyway, the story represents something much deeper.

The ancient Pecos spirit was alive and well, in spite of the efforts of generations of missionaries to undermine it. There was a comfort with the new faith and confidence in the mission system without fear of the terrible reprisals that would have punished the whole community in earlier years — and there were none. The sacred clown tradition that made fun of the holiest of events had not been suppressed. And these three days of laughter and fun raised the morale of the depressed people more than anything else could have done.

And the fact that Agustín was killed by (an apparent) bear for his efforts, guaranteed that his memory would last for generations.

Thanks to the Bishop, to Agustín, and the bear.

The Visitor — 1776

When roaming the ruins, I often wish for a time machine to transport me back to a particular era or event at this place. One of the next best things is to join Father Domínguez on his inspection tour in 1776.

Fray Francisco Atanasio Domínguez later co-led an expedition with Fray Silvestre Vélez de Escalante to the north and west of Santa Fe in a vain attempt to find a route to the Pacific. (Signs along the roadways now indicate the route of the Domínguez-Escalante expedition.) At the request of the royal governor and the provincial *custos* of the New Mexico missions, Domínguez observed and created detailed reports on each of the missions he visited.

He found that most of the missions were in sad shape. Buildings were falling down, the people were ill taught and neglected, the priests were too few and too many of them were totally dysfunctional. As a result of his input, mission conditions improved considerably over the next few years.

His description of Pecos is one of the best. Though only five pages long, it conveyed a lot of information.

Pecos had no priest at the time, the mission apparently not in use. One or more of the *fiscales* helped the people observe the rituals, teaching the children, leading rosaries in the church, and looking after mission affairs as much as possible. For baptisms, marriages, confessions or confirmations, the people had to travel to the parish church in Santa Fe, and it's not surprising that few did. They tended to burials in their own way.

The Pecos people were having trouble enough, what with Comanche raids, smallpox epidemics, and severe drought. Father Domínguez counted 100 families, some 269 persons, as the population had continued to decline from the 350 reported in 1760.

What did he see as he approached the pueblo? The long low ridge some seven leagues from Santa Fe, with the multistoried apartment blocks surrounding the main plaza at the north end; a long house block in the middle; and the church and *convento* looming at the south end. It must have been an awe-inspiring sight. Even in ruins, it still is.

He approached the church through the cemetery, its entrance to the west. He noted the two towers, one with a fine bell "given by the king" in it. A balcony and a square doorway set back a little bit stood between them. As he entered, he looked up at the choir loft directly overhead, and down the nave toward the altar. What he saw apparently pleased him.

He liked to count things. He measured the dimensions in *varas*, a little less than a yard, 51 in length, 9 wide. He counted the "finely wrought" roof beams with their carved corbels (one with Frater Carolus' name inscribed). Three windows on the south side, one on the north, one over the choir loft. A clerestory over the transept brought in light and air. A finely carved pulpit rose above the congregation on the right; a confessional and long bench stood opposite on the left. There were no pews: the people stood or kneeled on the dirt floor as directed by the *fiscales*.

Five steps with little railings on each side led up to the sanctuary. Behind the wooden altar, several paintings adorned the wall. One must have been the *Nuestra Señora de Los Ángeles* familiar to us today. Some of the others were old and blackened beyond recognition. A small crucifix, brass candlesticks, a lectern, two small bronze bells gleamed on the altar. Small doors at each side, with paintings above them, led to storerooms for church belongings. Each of the stubby arms at the transept crossing housed a plain wooden altar, at the moment bare and unadorned. More paintings were hung above them, some on ancient buffalo hide.

The interior of the church as described by Fr. Dominguez in 1775.

Doorways on the right led out to what was left of the old chapel constructed by Father Zeinos after the Pueblo Revolt. It occupied the space between the original church and *convento*, utilizing remaining walls from the original buildings. Though the structure was dilapidated and falling down, some portions were still in use. A small room at the west end held a baptismal font, and the long one running along to the east beside the wall of the new church served as the sacristy where objects needed for the mass were stored. Here Father Domínguez had a field day, opening drawers and cupboards and listing everything he found. Vestments, some of them two-sided in bright colors; altar cloths of fine linen; crosses large and small; communion ware, incense burners, processional candle holders, books and missals; molds for making communion bread; vials of holy oils; instruction from the Holy Office (the Inquisition) mounted on placards. Some things were chewed by rats, most still useful. He seemed disturbed that the few locks had no keys. Was thievery a problem?' There was no mention of communion wine. Had thirsty parishioners absconded with it?

Low stone and adobe walls mark what's left of the once-bustling, two story *convento*.

Large doors led him into the two-story *convento,* which he explored with delight (my interpretation). He spoke of the spacious porter's lodge, ten *varas* square with adobe benches built around three of the walls, and an unusual triple-arched roof. Two beautiful stables with straw lofts, the cloister, two stairways, the defensive *torreón* erected by the soldiers, a fine storeroom with no key to its door, a variety of other rooms both upstairs and downstairs, balconies looking out over the landscape. All caught his attention. He offered no description of the uses or furnishings of any of these rooms, nor of the large kitchen so prominent today, nor of any staff or supplies available. Some of the upstairs rooms were dilapidated and unusable; but for the most part, he seemed very pleased with the building, empty and abandoned as he made it sound. Was it? I want to know more.

His only mention of the *Casas Reales* was that someone had taken a balcony railing from the *convento* to put in it. This puzzles me, since he observed so much else so acutely. He probably stayed at the *Casas Reales* and was welcomed and fed by its residents, but we don't know. What did the building look like? How big was it? Who was there? How was it fortified against the Comanches? Though not part of his official assignment, I should think he would have said more about it, especially since one of his patrons was the royal governor and it served the people of the pueblo.

Outside, he walked over to inspect the mission croplands. Just west of the cemetery, he noted a fine, walled kitchen garden for greens and vegetables and fruit; but he didn't report if anyone was caring for it. No mention of orchards, pasturelands, paddocks, chicken coops, with or without occupants. On three sides were four large *milpas* (cornfields), one of which was irrigated. The Indians told him that corn and wheat were grown on these plots, but with no missionary in residence, they were cultivating them for themselves. Not surprising, but I wonder how Father Domínguez reacted. Probably very compassionately.

He was distressed by the condition of the Pecos Indians. The

Comanches had run off their once fine herds of horses, leaving them only a dozen "sorry nags." Their cattle had been reduced to eight old cows, until the governor had given them twelve more. (Were these cows used for milking, for eating, for manure, for hauling carts and plows, for their hides? All of the above? I want to know more.) Though the pueblo had fertile fields to the north and east, some of them irrigated, the Comanche raids had made it too dangerous to cultivate them. The Pecos River to the east had fine trout, but was far from the protection of the pueblo walls. Drought was severe, and the few crops harvested lasted only a few months of the year. Animals were few and far, and hunting was also limited. Wells had been dug near the foot of the ridge, but there is no mention of the creek running through the valley just to the west, which usually provided plenty of water. So the people were struggling for survival. Though some of them were good carpenters, or made pottery for the Hispanic settlers, or traded and crafted whatever they could, many had had to seek work elsewhere on ranches or in weaving rooms or tanning yards or wealthy kitchens for whatever sustenance they could earn. Father Domínguez described them as "*in puribus*, fugitives from their homes, absent from their families, selling those trifles they once bought to make themselves decent, on foot."

Apparently, neither the mission nor the government could help the Pecos people very much. They had not abandoned their traditional gods, who seemed to have abandoned them. Father Domínguez reported that there were nine active *kivas* at the pueblo, described by him as "chapter or council rooms, and the Indians meet in them, sometimes to discuss matters of their government for the coming year, their planting, arrangements for work to be done, to elect new community officials, to rehearse their dances, or sometimes for other things . . ."

Interesting. Were the Indians able to conceal their sacred rituals and the deeper significance of the *kivas* from inquiring Spaniards? Was Father Domínguez really unaware of the religious focus of the *kivas* that so many missionaries had tried to obliterate? Or was he in full knowledge of these things and through his bland, secular description, trying in his own way to protect these people who had lost so much?

Now, the ruins of the great pueblo are just mounds of earth. The once beautiful church is a roofless cluster of tall, red, eroding walls. The bustling *convento* rooms are marked with low stone outlines. The *Casas Reales* is totally invisible, not even acknowledged with a sign.

But walking around in the imaginary company of Father Domínguez, his observations help my mind envision what he might have seen in that beautiful place. My questions and comments bombard him, and sometimes answers and insights emerge from deep within my memory where forgotten information from many sources is stored. And our dialogue deepens, and enriches.

He's inviting us, you as well as me. Let's go.

The Peace of Pecos

One of the strangest events in the life of the mission occurred on March 1, 1786.

During the early 1700s, the Comanches had migrated from the north to the Southern Plains. As horse people, they roamed freely in search of the buffalo that sustained them. Their fierce warriors preyed upon other tribes and increasingly raided the Spanish settlements and Pueblo communities along the Rio Grande and its tributaries.

Pecos, as the easternmost pueblo on the pass through the mountains between the Great Plains and the valley of the Rio Grande, was a frequent target. Again and again, masses of Comanche warriors swept in undetected, killed, looted, grabbed captives, destroyed crops, ran off the pueblo horse herds, and dashed away again unscathed. Understandably, the Pecos people were nervous. Though a handful of government soldiers was stationed at the pueblo and had built the defensive *torreón* in the *convento*, the raids were so sudden and devastating that the soldiers and the diminishing number of Pecos warriors could seldom respond effectively.

When veteran soldier Juan Bautista de Anza was

appointed Governor of New Mexico, he vowed to change all that. He led a large force of government soldiers and militia made up of settlers and pueblo auxiliaries far out on the plains where they ambushed a huge camp of Comanches on their own ground. They killed and captured many and scattered the rest. Among the dead was the most dreaded Comanche chief, Cuerno Verde (*Green Horn*, so named for the painted buffalo headdress he favored). A major victory for the Spaniards and major blow to the Comanches.

That was in August 1779. A few years later, due to this and a number of other complex factors, the Comanches were eager for peace with the Spaniards. Emissaries went back and forth between their camps on the plains and Santa Fe. As details were hammered out. Pecos was agreed upon as the treaty site.

It was mid-February, not the best time for traveling in wintery New Mexico. Imagine the consternation of the Pecos people huddled within their sheltering walls as they saw hundreds of Comanche tipis being set up on the trading field below the pueblo. Had these fierce enemies really come in peace, or was this just a ploy disguising another brutal raid?

A delegation of Comanche leaders in their finest regalia followed Ecueracapa (*Leather Cape*), designated spokesman for all the Comanche bands, over the mountains to Santa Fe. Extravagantly welcomed by Governor Anza, for four days the guests were lavishly fêted while negotiations went on. Anza and his retinue joined them for the ride back to Pecos, where he submitted to embraces and flowery speeches from many of the two hundred Comanches remaining at their camp. (His ribs must have been sore afterwards.)

The next day, February 28, 1786, the actual ceremonies were performed. Long speeches, ritual smoking of pipes, gifts, a symbolic "burying of war" between them, quantities of food, festivities. The Comanches promised no longer to raid Spanish settlements nor Pueblo communities, and were granted access to Santa Fe, free trading at Pecos, annual distribution of gifts, and other special privileges. Ecueracapa was named Captain General of all the Comanches and given a sword, a banner, and a Governor's staff of office. It was a grand event full of symbolism.

The out-of-season trade fair the next day was a more-or-less completely honest one. Fair exchanges were listed (so many blankets for a horse or a captive, so many steel knives for a buffalo robe). Every transaction was overseen by monitors appointed by the Governor. Usually the trade-sharp Pecos and settlers swindled and cheated the more naïve Comanches mercilessly, perhaps a small retaliation for the terror of the raids. The era of peace had begun, with good feelings throughout.

March 1 was Ash Wednesday on the Christian calendar, usually a solemn occasion as the first day of Lent, the time of fasting and repentance. The descriptions I have read merely mention that the Comanches voluntarily joined the Spanish governor and staff at the mass, receiving the ashes on their heads. But just imagine it.

The priest surely felt pressure under the circumstances to make the occasion as splendid as possible, in spite of the somberness of the liturgical ritual. Picture the dim interior of the mission church, the same one whose walls can still embrace us, sparkling with candles and color, saints and shining vessels, with *Nuestra Señora de Los Ángeles* presiding over all from her painting above the altar. Picture the priest in his vestments, a cross gleaming on his chest, directing his Christian convert helpers. Look and listen to the choir, instrumentalists (trumpet? violin? guitar? organ? all possible.), ringers of big and little bells, youngsters carrying tall candles in procession and swinging pots of incense, the liturgists crying out the sacred words while interpreters struggled to rephrase the messages in Towa (the Pecos language) as well as Comanche. Listen to the homily. What would the priest have said on this special occasion? Watch the drama of the mass as light streamed in from the clerestory in the roof and music reechoed from the thick adobe walls.

Here were Indians, *mestizos, genízaros,* pueblos, settlers, Spanish officials, crowded together under this roof. Ecueracapa and his Comanches in their feathers and finery. Governor Anza and his staff with their ribbons and medals and symbols of office. The Pecos leaders and their blanket-wrapped people. Soldiers and settlers and Indians visiting from other tribes. Former enemies, wary allies, elbow to elbow, filling the church and overflowing outside. Whether or not they understood the theology, the ashes of repentance and renewal on each forehead bound them together in the promise of peace and a new era under the cross of Cristo and the watchful gaze of his mother.

The Peace of Pecos held for generations. The Comanches came and went, traded freely, assisted the New Mexicans in conflicts with other tribes, protected the hunters and travelers out on the plains, and became trusted friends and allies. Without fear of the Comanche raids, Spanish settlers in ever greater numbers moved into the Pecos valley, developing their ranches and communities in peace, gradually displacing the diminishing population of Pecos Pueblo. (The descendents of the Spanish settlers are still here.)

Interlude

In 1838, the tiny handful of Pecos Pueblo residents picked up their belongings, their children, and whatever sacred objects they could carry and moved away. They crossed the mountains to the Pueblo of Jemez some eighty miles to the west. This was the only other pueblo that also spoke their ancestral language, Towa.

Disease, smallpox, out-migration, and just plain discouragement had reduced their numbers to about twenty, although accounts vary. It was no longer a viable community. Crops, ceremonies, and the house blocks were neglected for lack of "hands." The traditional culture was crumbling, as well as the buildings. A priest, now stationed at San Miguel del Vado, seldom came to celebrate mass any more, and the church itself was deteriorating.

Since the Peace of Pecos with the Comanches in 1786, Hispanic settlers in greater numbers had been moving into the valley. They set up homesteads and *ranchos* and new villages all along the river, and some of the Pecos Indians had joined their communities. Though much of the pueblo land was protected by law, many farmers were grazing animals or raising crops on land the

Pecos were too few to utilize, and the people had little energy to resist them. The final decision to move away was inevitable, but it must have been extremely difficult to leave behind the heritage of generations.

In 1821, when Mexico gained its independence from Spain, traders from Missouri and the American East were welcome in New Mexico. The Santa Fe Trail brought great freight wagons, swift stagecoaches and strange Anglo people passing close to the pueblo, sometimes camping beside traditional pueblo springs. The ruined pueblo had a great fascination for the travelers. In the early years, some commented sadly about the few blanket-wrapped figures standing on rooftops gazing off into the distance as if looking for their past glories. Others explored the ruins, particularly after the inhabitants had left, gathering up as souvenirs whatever had been left behind.

Fantastic stories circulated — this was the Victorian era, remember, when romantic sentimentalism was the norm.

Montezuma himself had lived at the pueblo, they said, and before he left for Aztec Mexico, he lit a sacred fire that the people tended carefully for generations awaiting his return.

A huge sacred serpent had lived in one of the *kivas* (or maybe a nearby cave) and ate sacrificed babies. When there were no more babies, the serpent went away in a huff and the community died.

In 1839, Journalist Matt Field from the New Orleans *Picayune* wrote of an ancient goatherd who lived in the church. He shared with Matt his porridge of corn meal and goat milk by torchlight at the foot of the altar and told a romantic story about a pair of lovers who died in each other's arms in the last flames of the sacred fire. In that setting, Field was willing to believe anything, particularly when the old man presented him with a couple of cinders left over from that conflagration.

The church continued to be a source of wonder. In 1846, Susan Shelby Magoffin in her diary wrote that she was "truly awed." The beautifully carved woodwork remaining, even though "battered," showed that if the people "were uncivilized or half civilized as we generally believe them, they had at least an idea of grandeur." Many visitors made drawings of the ruined "Aztec Temple" in various degrees of dilapidation, more romantic than realistic, though they had very little knowledge of the people who had lived there.

After the pueblo people left, some Hispanic settlers made themselves at home in the habitable parts of the house blocks for a while. They plowed up the old trading field for crops and brought their cattle down from the mountains to graze there in the winters. In 1842, Mexican soldiers captured, or rescued, the lost and starving remnants of the Texas expedition that was out to annex New Mexico. They housed the survivors in the pueblo ruins for a couple of days and tore down much of the roofing and woodwork for firewood. In both the Mexican and Civil wars, soldiers camped nearby and helped along the destruction. In the late 1850s, with official permission, Martin Kozlowski removed roof beams from the church to use in the trading post he was building nearby, opening up the walls to further erosion. The site became a favorite day-trip picnic destination for Santa Feans, who delighted in the "romance of the ruins," as well as the fine scenery surrounding them.

By 1880, the once-great city had been reduced to piles of rubble. That year, the railroad came through the valley. Conductors and a huge sign pointed out the red walls of the old church and the rubbly hillocks where the pueblo had stood. They still can be seen from the train. That same year, the Swiss archaeologist Adolph Bandelier examined the ruins and made an accurate guess about the structure of the pueblo. "I have at last found my true calling," he is said to have exulted from this experience, and he went on to a notable career in Southwest archaeology and ethnology.

Meanwhile, what was happening to the Pecos descendants? At Jemez, they were welcomed, given housing and farmland. Though incorporated into that community, they maintained their identity and shared some of their traditions and beliefs. They flourished, gradually becoming a substantial segment of the Jemez population. Eventually, the federal government recognized them as an independent tribe affiliated with Jemez, with their own governor looking out for their interests.

As for the homeland they had left behind, they didn't just give it up. Though they had once controlled the whole northern part of the Pecos Valley, legally they still owned "four leagues," i.e. one league in each direction measured from the cross—now disappeared—in front of the church. This came to some 27 square miles, much of it prime real estate. The legal tangles over the years as they tried to reclaim it, sell it, or make use of it were confusingly complex, in and out of law courts, passing from one official owner to another, confounded by government wobbling about the legal status of the tribe and its rights to the land. According to the decision in 1959, the Pecos descendants have no more official claim to their ancestral lands.

But many of them return frequently to their old homeland, young and old, with school classes, in family groups, with senior outings. They connect with the welcoming Park staff, help care for the artifacts in the lab, preside at certain ceremonies. They worship at secret shrines in the area, gather the memories of their elders, study the exhibits in the museum, share the old stories with their children. Potters, weavers, jewelry makers demonstrate their work to visitors. And of course, others just want to hang out in this beautiful place. Yes, Pecos descendants are still here—the living among the ancestors.

In 1915, a new phase of the Pecos Story began. Scientific archaeology entered the picture. Before this time, Southwest archaeology had been basically glorified pot hunting, the archeologists seeking specimens for Eastern museums. But Dr. Alfred Vincent Kidder from the R.S. Peabody Foundation in Andover, Massachusetts, wanted to understand more about the structure of the pueblo and the lives of the people who had lived there. Between 1915 and 1929, his workers excavated portions of the midden, the dump sloping along the eastern edge of the ridge from the pueblo to the trading field. Based on the thousands of pottery shards unearthed in the different strata, he established the first chronology of pueblo development anywhere in the Southwest. Digging into some of the room blocks around the main plaza and other nearby ruins, he studied construction methods and the domestic patterns of generations of ancient residents. He uncovered many burials, which he sent off to Harvard for analysis, and eventually backfilled the ruins for their protection and preservation, creating the great mounds we see there today.

The wall in front of the picture marks the foundations of the "old" church. Compare them with the visible walls of the "new" one.

About the same time in 1915, Jesse Nusbaum of the Museum of New Mexico began excavations and stabilization of the old mission church. His workers removed tons of debris, rebuilt the collapsed back wall and strengthened the foundations. Underneath the original floor, which they replaced, they found skeletons of many unidentified individuals, presumably most of them Christian Indians who had been interred in this sacred space. (Agustín Guichi was said to have been buried here.) The only two wooden coffins enclosed the remains of two priests dressed in their robes. I wonder who they were. The archaeologists reburied these individuals elsewhere, and they left the church looking much as it does today.

The beams protruding from the walls are original. When the light is right some carvings can be seen on some of them. The back wall was reconstructed because the original had collapsed.

All this attention led to a complex series of sales and deeds. In 1935, the ruins came under protection as a State Monument; and in 1965, it was elevated to a National Monument under the care of the National Park Service. But it wasn't until 1967 that, under the supervision of Jean

Pinkley, excavations revealed the foundations of Father Andrés Juárez' enormous church embracing the foundations of the later one.

One surprise. The archaeologist found a kiva in the remains of the *convento*. What was it doing there?

Several theories emerged. The Franciscans were skilled at co-opting alien symbols for their own purposes. Perhaps an enterprising friar (Fr. Andres?) had filled the kiva with saints instead of *kachinas*, teaching the faith in surroundings familiar to his listeners. Possibly, after the Pueblo Revolt, in defiance of the Christian teachings, some of the Pecos had simply reclaimed their sacred space in the heart of the mission. And, later perhaps returning missionaries had filled the kiva with sand, effectively destroying and concealing it for generations. Speculations abound.

The restored kiva is one of two at the Park you can enter.

In 1990, with the addition of much more land donated by Greer Garson Fogelson, the Pecos Monument became a National Historical Park. Now it has a fine visitor center, film and museum, an interpretive trail through the ruins of the pueblo and mission, a Civil War battlefield, Greer Garson's ranch, and programs that help visitors learn about the people who used to live in this place.

It's true that the old church looks like a dramatic wreck. Every winter storms, ice and wind threaten to crumble its red walls to dust. Every summer, crews work to repair the damage to the church and the *convento*. The church, even in its roofless state, is a site for many special events, from weddings to Feast Day Mass to Christmas Posadas, and more.

When you visit the park, step into the church, listen quietly, and perhaps you'll sense the vibes of long-ago events emanating from the ancient adobe walls.

The Pecos Feast Days

The early Franciscan missionaries brought with them a special veneration for *Nuestra Señora de Los Ángeles de Porciúncula* Our Lady of the Angels) from the little chapel (Porciuncula) where Saint Francis began his ministry. This saint, *Nuestra Señora*, was assigned to the large and prosperous Pecos Pueblo, which dominated the pass between the Great Plains and the Rio Grande valley.

The first painting of the saint was placed over the altar of the huge church completed about 1625, but it was destroyed along with the church in the Pueblo Revolt of 1680.

Another painting, brought from Mexico, was hung above the altar of the later church completed about 1717. From there, she watched over the community, cared for the people in good times and bad, blessed those who came to her with love in their hearts. She was part of the living spirit of the Pecos Pueblo.

Just before the last handful of pueblo residents left in 1838, they took the picture to Saint Anthony's church in the small Hispanic village nearby. Please, they requested, keep this picture for us, hang it in a prominent place in your church, and celebrate our annual feast day on our behalf.

The picture can still be seen in that church, and her feast day is celebrated each year in the ruins of the old mission church of Pecos Pueblo.

The interactions between the missionaries and the native people were very complex, leading to much interweaving of the traditional pueblo beliefs and the faith of the Catholic missionaries. As a result, the Pecos descendents honor both their Native and Spanish Christian heritages at the time of the Feast of *Nuestra Señora de Los Ángeles* the first week in August.

On August 2, the whole community of Jemez Pueblo honors the saint with an ancient corn dance. Hundreds of people, the Turquoise and the Squash clans alternating, fill the Jemez Plaza. The men are dressed in white dance kilts with foxtails swishing behind, the women in black *mantas* with symbolic *tablitas* attached to their heads. With rattles picking up the rhythm and sprigs of evergreen waving in their hands, the elders lead the procession, and the little children follow the lines of dancers as best they can. The throbbing of the drums, the deep voices of the singers and the precise movements of the dancers create a spiritual ritual with awesome power.

The Pecos Bull, a tradition brought from the old homeland, cavorts merrily. The Bull is a large contraption of burlap painted with black circles. A long neck and small head adorn one end and a rope tail the other. The legs of its bearer are visible underneath. It is led by a rider prancing ahead with a cute little horse figure attached to his body. The discordant rat-a-tat-tat of a snare drum competes sharply with the rhythm of the big pueblo drums. Whiteface cowboys follow along, entangling each other and unwary visitors with long whips and lassos, while the bull goes charging among the dancers and spectators to the great delight of everybody. This is part of the Sacred Clown tradition that enlivens many pueblo ceremonies.

Pueblo hospitality on such feast days is lavish. Great feasts are spread in many homes, which friends and lucky visitors are invited to share. The preparations for the day are immense, for everything must be done just right in honor of *Nuestra Señora* and in harmony with the spirits of past and present. Most visitors find the feast day celebration a powerful experience, as their respectful presence and prayers intensify the spiritual energies of the dancers and as they share the abundance of the earth with their hosts. Faith and food, the dance and generosity, as in so many religious settings, unite diverse people in a sense of shared community.

The first Sunday in August, the congregation of St. Anthony's in Pecos honors the Spanish side of the Pecos Pueblo heritage. A solemn procession walks the three miles from the church in the village to the Park and joins the larger crowd gathered there for the entrance into the ruins of the old church. Guitars strike up and the choir sings hymns in Spanish, English and Latin. A cross and banners lead the way, as honored bearers carry the image of *Nuestra Señora* and hang the picture (now a reproduction) on its spike above the flower bedecked temporary altar in the roofless ruins. Chairs fill the nave, and several hundred people celebrate the festive mass, many sheltering under colorful umbrellas from the sun or occasional showers. Guitars throb, voices soar, incense wafts through the air, holy water sprinkles blessings upon the faithful. The white-robed priest and his helpers lead the ancient liturgies that have resounded between these crumbling walls over the centuries with words of hope and faith and love. The mystery of the bread and wine, the body and blood of Christ, the food that strengthens the spirit and unites his people everywhere, is shared by all who choose.

The Pecos Pueblo Governor, bearing the official cane of office presented by President Lincoln in the 1860s, brings greetings, and spiritual leaders offer long prayers in Towa, the ancestral language of this place. Under the gaze of *Nuestra Señora*, the drama of the Christian faith that forever changed the lives of the Pecos Pueblo people is reenacted once again in this sacred space.

Afterwards, everybody gathers in the nearby picnic area. Women have been baking sweet rolls and cookies in the traditional beehive *horno* there and preparing buckets of lemonade. Guitars and singers continue their traditional Hispanic music in the background, as folks meet and mingle and share conversation and food. It is a joyful, mellow time with its own ancient spirit and sense of community gathered in honor of *Nuestra Señora de Los Ángeles* that reverberates down through the centuries.

Visitors are welcome at both of these events, and their prayers and presence intensify the spiritual dimensions of each.

Return of the Ancestors

Human remains. Burials. Skeletons. Honored Ancestors. The adventures of some of the Pecos Old Ones continued long after their deaths.

When Dr. Kidder excavated portions of the midden and some of the house blocks, he found burials. Hundreds of them. Over the ten-year project (1915–1929 with time out for World War One), he unearthed and shipped off to Harvard University some two thousand skeletons, neatly categorized according to the strata in which they were found, along with their accompanying grave goods.

The physical anthropologists at Harvard's Peabody Museum were delighted with this immense treasure. Here was a virtual history of a community over the course of centuries. There was nothing like it anywhere.

And what stories the bones told. The eager examiners learned about periods of plenty and times of famine. They could detect signs of various diseases that swept through the pueblo and when warfare left bashed skulls and projectile points imbedded in bone. They could see where broken bones had healed and where skillful surgery had opened skulls with obsidian chisels — and the patients had survived. They could chart the wear and tear on the joints caused by hard and heavy work, and the physical effect of changing technologies, some brought by the Spanish colonists. They could sympathize with the ravages of the arthritis that afflicted many, and the broken teeth that caused often-fatal abscesses. They could lament with families the many deaths of babies and children, and rejoice with those few who lived into their sixties. They could identify, in many cases, people from other tribes who may have come for trade or protection, as slaves or immigrants, or just to visit with the hospitable Pecos people, for their physical build was different. They admired the pottery, the tools, the baskets or bits of woven textiles, the jewelry and other objects buried with the deceased. They found a sturdy people who survived as well as those in any other part of the world throughout the 13th to 18th centuries. And some of them emerged as distinct individuals.

Of course I'm assuming, perhaps mistakenly, that the investigators were looking at "people," not just "specimens."

Reports were written and further studies undertaken, including a major one about osteoporosis. Then the bones, remains of cherished people, were stashed in boxes in the basement. There they languished, seldom looked at, for 85 years.

Until 1999.

Why had these loved ones been buried in the midden, the dump?
> The earth near the pueblo is very hard and difficult to dig with the tools then available. Softer ground near the streams and springs was needed for farming. But the midden, at the foot of the community, had evolved into a long slope of earth and debris that was easy to excavate. There the deceased who were placed lovingly in narrow unmarked graves could find rest.

Why didn't the Pecos descendants protest their removal when it was happening?
> Jemez was far away. Transportation and communication were

difficult. The slowly growing Pecos population was having enough problems with mere survival. And besides, in those days, nobody paid much attention to Indians anyway.

Why did the archaeologists desecrate the graves in that way?

In that era, human remains, particularly Indian ones, were dug up everywhere, scattered around and displayed in museums. (Peruvian mummies are still popular exhibits.) Some archaeologists piled up bones for mug shots in ways that dismay us nowadays. But to the credit of Kidder & Co., the Pecos burials were treated with care and respect, for what they could teach as well as for what they were.

Are more excavations of the pueblo ruins planned?

No. There are too many burials throughout the area, probably thousands of them. The house block mounds and the midden are sacred sites, conserved and honored for the spirits of the ancestors still there.

In 1990, under increasing pressure from the Indian Sovereignty Movement, Congress passed the Native American Graves Protection and Repatriation Act known as NAGPRA. It mandated that every institution that receives government funding must return human remains, grave goods and sacred objects to their original tribes if requested. This started a mad scramble, as museums and universities struggled to sort out what they had in their collections, affiliated with which tribes, how to make contact with appropriate Indian leaders, and which items they might want returned.

The increasingly influential Pecos/Jemez community was at the forefront of this movement. But the process took almost ten years because materials excavated from Pecos were scattered among many museums from Boston to Tucson, and often mixed in haphazardly with objects from other tribes. Spiritual and political leaders had to be invited to examine everything to determine what they wanted returned and how they planned to care for each item. And it was complicated by the fact that every January 6, a new governing council takes over at Jemez, which meant that many delicate negotiations had to start over again.

Of course, the Pecos people wanted their ancestors returned. And of course, Harvard didn't want to let them go and only agreed to relinquish them after considerable persuasion. After countless negotiations, conflicts, compromises, delays, and patient building of relationships by many people, everything was arranged. The ancestors would return to their ancient homeland, cared for by the National Park Service in coordination with the Pecos elders.

A contingent of Pecos spiritual and political leaders went to Harvard University in Massachusetts where they officially received the ancestral remains with ancient prayers and ceremonies. The remains were loaded in a huge panel truck for the trip across the country, escorted by Jemez Pueblo police and National Park rangers.

At that time, hundreds of Pecos/Jemez people and friends began the three-day hike over ancient trails from Jemez back to their old homeland, retracing the route their forefathers had taken when they left the pueblo in 1838. Old folks hobbled along on the arms of their children; youngsters and kids scampered over the paths; mothers lugged babies in their backpacks; teenagers ran and leapt over logs and rocks and gullies; men and women in jeans and hiking boots took leave of their jobs; pueblo leaders carried their official canes of office. It was an amazing human reverse-migration that was hosted overnights at Cochiti Pueblo and the Santa Fe Indian School. For many participants, it was an intense spiritual experience.

At dawn on May 22nd, the hikers and many others met the truck at the entrance to the Park. Prayers and ceremonies welcomed the ancestors now reunited with their community. Newspaper photographs show the procession into the Park. It was led by Pecos Pueblo leaders wearing white trousers, brightly-colored ribbon shirts, turquoise jewelry and colorful headbands, followed by the truck and a stream of Indian people stretching back as far as one could see.

The Park staff had prepared a mass gravesite in the back country where it would not be disturbed. Only the Pecos descendants were permitted at the burial itself, where the ancestors, all two thousand plus of them, were removed from their storage boxes and returned to Mother Earth with appropriate prayers and ceremonies.

Afterwards, everybody, including me, gathered at the picnic area parking lot near the ruins of the old mission church. It was estimated that some fifteen hundred people, mostly Indians in their best, most colorful clothes, were sitting around under the trees, shaded by their umbrellas, or out in the hot sun. A platform had been set up in the parking lot, on which special guests perched on folding chairs. The loudspeaker system actually worked, carrying the speakers' voices loud and clear. Holy men offered prayers in the ancient Towa language and in Spanish. The Jemez drum group honored the walkers. Speakers from everywhere included officials from Washington and Santa Fe; representatives of the Bureau of Indian Affairs and the National Park Service; many Indian tribal leaders; directors of museums and NAGPRA; local clergy and politicians; those who had worked tirelessly to make possible this repatriation. The speeches were pertinent and mercifully brief, while journalists and even a photographer from *The National Geographic* recorded the event.

And then something amazing happened. Just as the last speaker was concluding his remarks, from an almost clear sky a great roar of thunder shivered the air. I could see heads ducking in alarm and eyes searching skyward to seek its source. Immediately, a whirlwind picked up dust and gravel from the unpaved parking lot and slung it all around. I could see people's hands, like mine, raised to protect their faces. Then silence. Calm. Peace.

People raised their heads with great smiles shining forth as they patted their neighbors. "That's it. That's the sign. Just as predicted by the elders. The ancestors are speaking. They are saying they are glad to be home again, and thanks to all who have helped bring them here."

No matter what one believes—or doesn't—this was one of those powerfully unforgettable moments, in the shadow of the ancient mission church (metaphorically speaking, because the sun actually cast the shadow in another direction) that unites the spirits of past and present in a moment of eternity.

A huge feast that had been prepared over several days by busy pueblo women followed, along with mellow sociability and cheerful interactions while the drum group thumped and sang in the background. Eventually, the crowd dispersed, the people drifting away to their separate homes, knowing that they had participated in something very special.

The gravesite is off limits to Park visitors, unmarked and accessible only to Park rangers and Pecos descendants. Electronic sensors protect the area from vandals or casual intrusion and were initially set so sensitively that a passing coyote or rabbit set them off, rousing rangers from their beds to investigate. A Pecos man who visited the site a year after the burial told me with amazement that, though the ground around it was hard and bare, the grave itself was thickly covered with little purple flowers. And occasionally, I have seen a Pecos visitor walking nearby taking a pinch of sacred corn meal from a little pouch and scattering it in the direction of the ancestors' resting place.

What does all this have to do with the mission itself? For me, many things, and it symbolizes a lot.

Many of these returned ancestors had related to the mission in one way or another in every degree and combination of acceptance, wariness, delight, indifference, hostility, gratitude and misgivings. They had served, endured, welcomed, resisted, profited by, rejected and protected the many missionaries along with what they brought and represented. They are an essential part of the mission story.

Partly because of these ancestors and what they revealed to the archaeologists and anthropologists, the ruins of the pueblo and the mission were deemed important enough for state and federal protection and are still teaching countless visitors about the rich heritage they represent.

Because of or in spite of them, depending on your point of view, the Pecos people survive, their traditions largely intact with a blending of Christian and ancient beliefs and practices passed down from these ancestors, that influence lives to this day.

And the spirits of these ancestors, whether Christianized or not, unite past and present, and have not lost their power.

May they rest in peace.

As seen from the upper parking lot, the *convento* ruins spread out on this side of the mission church.

Sources And Notes

Books:

As I mentioned earlier, by far the best resource is:

Kiva, Cross and Crown: The Pecos Indians and New Mexico 1540-1840, by John Kessell (1979, University of New Mexico Press; 2nd edition 1987). I have cited it often in these pages.

Other pertinent books include:

Pecos: Gateway to Pueblos and Plains. An anthology of interesting articles by various authors, compiled by the staff of Southwest Parks and Monuments Association, published by SPMA in 1988. This follows the history of the park as displayed in the museum and includes many of the fine illustrations found there.

The Four Churches of Pecos. Alden C. Hayes (1974, University of New Mexico Press). An archaeologist's account of the excavations of churches and *convento* in 1966. Interesting in many ways, and also infuriating because of mislabeling—or non-labeling—of pertinent diagrams. He mentions the *Casas Reales*, its dimensions generally outlined, but only a couple of small rooms were excavated then and the rest of it is still waiting for attention.

The Missions of New Mexico. 1776, as described by Fray Francisco Atanasio Domínguez. Translated and Annotated by Eleanor B. Adams and Fray Angélico Chávez (New Edition, Sunstone Press: Santa Fe, 2012. Originally published for the Cultural Properties Review Committee and the State Planning Office, by University of New Mexico Press in 1976). The section on Pecos, pp 209-214, has been cited by many authors, and his descriptions of the church are the basis of the wayside signs at the park.

El Camino Real de Tierra Adentro. Another fine anthology about the traffic along the route from Mexico City to Santa Fe, published by the Bureau of Land Management in two volumes, in 1993 and 1999. Many interesting articles by different people about the caravans and the goods brought for missions and for the settlers.

Pecos, New Mexico: Archaeological Notes. Alfred Vincent Kidder (1958, published by the Robert S. Peabody Foundation for Archaeology at Phillips Academy in Andover, Massachusetts). A retrospective account of the excavations at Pecos Pueblo between 1915 and 1929, much more readable than many archaeological reports, written with humanity and humility. His descriptions of the burials found under the church floor are particularly poignant.

The Golden Empire by Hugh Thomas. "Spain, Charles V, and the Creation of America" (2010, Random House) Story of the development of the Americas during the reign of Charles V (1522–66). Excellent, readable, much of relevance to New Mexico.

Added to these are countless books and articles read over the years about the history and anthropology of New Mexico not listed here. Many of them refer to Pecos in passing. In spite of frequent bias, all add various dimensions to the larger picture. The pueblo people have been favorite targets of anthropologists, though their oral histories and religious beliefs are still carefully guarded secrets.

Other sources of information include many personal conversations and observations that are not listed here.

Notes

Fray Luis:

More about related context, in Kessell, pp. 25-27

The Mission Builder:

Kessell writes a lot about Father Andrés: pp 115-138,152, 167, 170. We share considerable admiration for the man.

Regarding the supply caravans, several articles provide interesting descriptions in El Camino Real.

An archaeologist, in personal conversation, told me that there had been very little research on the actual building of the New Mexico missions—construction methods, work crews, outside assistance, relationships with the people during the process. Some Indians insist they were built by slave labor, under the whip, but I don't believe it. Forced labor would have created bad vibes detrimental to worship and to gathering local and regional converts. It was against the Laws of the Indies to enslave or overwork the native people; payment of some kind was mandated for work; and the Pecos people, being tough traders, would have insisted on the best deal for their workers. In addition, Father Andrés was apparently a humane and caring individual, much respected by Indians and others.

The People Divided:
There are many descriptions of the Pueblo Revolt, including the Pecos involvement in the rebellion and the return.
The story of Father Zeinos is told in most detail in Kessell, pp 272-281.

Renewal and Decline.
The "Frater Carolus" carved on a beam in the church was observed by Father Domínguez. Kessell searched out further information about the man, reported on pp 305-307, 334. His written page with the strawberries is reproduced on p. 306.
Kessell's list of the Pecos missionaries is on pp 498-503.

The Two Bishops:
This story is recounted, with variations, in many places. In Kessell, pp 336-341.

The Visitor:
Domínguez' account is fascinating, and irritating (to me) because of all the things he has left out. But I do walk around the ruins sometimes in his imaginary company, "listening," arguing and demanding more of his observations.

The Peace of Pecos:
Of the several accounts I have read, only Kessell describes the events of the peace ceremonies themselves. He mentions the Ash Wednesday service, but the elaborations on the mass are my own. Which priest at Pecos in 1786 presided, the "notorious drunkard" Jose de Burgos, or Francisco de Hozio, "long-time presidia chaplain at Santa Fe"? Was the

mission still able to provide the choirs and processions I've imagined? Dunno. But sounds possible.

Interlude:

Many travelers along the Santa Fe Trail commented on the Pecos ruins. The ones cited here are Matt Field, a journalist for the New Orleans Picayune, reporting in 1839; the other Susan Shelby Magoffin, a young bride traveling with her trader husband in 1846.

Matt Field. On The Santa Fe Trail. John Sunder, Ed., U. of Oklahoma Press, 1960, pp. 247-251.

The Diary of Susan Shelby Magoffin, 1846–1847. Stella M. Drummond, Ed., U. of Nebraska Press, Reprint 1982, pp. 99-102.

Re control of the Pecos homeland, the complex negotiations are well summarized in Kessell, pp 465-471.

Return of the Ancestors:

I knew many of the key people involved in the repatriation efforts and observed the process over several years. I was present in Andover for ceremonies returning some sacred objects to the Pecos elders (not the human remains: they came from Harvard) and again at the ceremonies at the Park a couple of days later. Though the actual burial of the remains was off limits to outsiders, the event was a very moving experience.

www.ingramcontent.com/pod-product-compliance
Lightning Source LLC
Chambersburg PA
CBHW051659040426
42446CB00009B/1218